Inspiring Leadership:
Character and Ethics Matter

Inspiring Leadership:
Character and Ethics Matter

R. Stewart Fisher
Perry J. Martini

BRANDON —

BEST OF LUCK IN YOUR PURSUITS
AFTER HIGH SCHOOL. REMEMBER THAT
CHARACTER & ETHICS DO MATTER —

AN ACADEMY LEADERSHIP BOOK

Printed in the United States of America.

Academy Leadership books are available at special quantity discounts to use as premiums and sales promotions, or for use in corporate training programs. For more information, please call Academy Leadership at 866-783-0630, or write to: 10120 Valley Forge Circle, King of Prussia, PA 19406 USA.

ISBN 0-9727323-2-2
Library of Congress Control Number: 2004112527

DEDICATED TO THE BRAVE MEN AND WOMEN OF OUR ARMED
FORCES WHO HAVE ANSWERED THE CALL OF ENDURING FREEDOM
TO PROTECT AND DEFEND FREEDOM-LOVING PEOPLE THROUGHOUT
THE WORLD IN THE WAR ON TERROR.

Contents

Foreword   i

Introduction   iii

Acknowledgments   ix

PART I
Character and Ethics: They Do Matter

Chapter 1   Ethics   1

Chapter 2   Integrity   9

Chapter 3   Truth   19

Chapter 4   Honor, Courage, and Commitment   29

Chapter 5   Patriotism   43

PART II
Advanced Leadership: Traits That Inspire Winning Teams

Chapter 6   Fidelity and Obedience   57

Chapter 7   Communication   65

Chapter 8   Empowerment   81

Chapter 9   Decisiveness   97

Chapter 10   Fairness and Consistency   113

Chapter 11   Patience, Perseverance, and Adaptability   127

PART III
The Golden Rule:
"Do Unto Others, As You Would Have Them Do Unto You"

Chapter 12   Servant Leadership   141

Chapter 13   Humility   155

Chapter 14   Example   169

Chapter 15   Love and Friendship   185

Chapter 16   Dignity, Decency, and Respect   201

Chapter 17   Faith, Spirit, and Spiritual Roots   215

Epilogue   231

Endnotes   235

Name Index   241

Foreword

It was my distinct privilege to serve as a naval officer during World War II. I quickly saw that the Navy believed in the very same values I learned from my father, Joshua Wooden, so many years ago on our Indiana farm: character, ethics, honor, courage, and commitment.

On a ship at sea, the captain has ultimate authority and accountability. If his ship runs aground, whether he was on the bridge at the time or not, he is still at fault, for it is his responsibility to train every officer and sailor serving under him. Accountability is a cornerstone of leadership. The Navy instills this principle in all of its men and women, and it is a valuable lesson for anyone who wants to become a great leader, whether in the service or civilian life.

Yet today, that sense of responsibility and accountability is often lacking in our leaders. Too many people are playing the "blame game" and pointing their fingers at others when they should be looking at themselves. They have forgotten Harry Truman's axiom, "The buck stops here." Human beings have the precious gift of free will, and therefore, the ability to choose. Who we become is the result of those choices, not the fault of someone else.

This principle and so many others that my dad and the Navy taught me are universal and timeless. In other words, they apply in both military and civilian life, in all ages, and across all cultures.

Captain Stew Fisher and Captain Perry Martini have written a marvelous book that captures the "true essence" of great leadership and resonates with the themes in my own books, especially *Wooden: A Lifetime of Reflections On and Off the Court*. Using riveting accounts of the most influential leaders in history, they remind us that inspiring leadership has its foundation in character and ethics. Without those roots, great leadership is impossible. Stew and Perry show us why leaders such as Abraham Lincoln and Mother Teresa changed the world.

They also remind us that our Founding Fathers believed in Judeo-Christian values. In order for this fledgling democracy to work, it relied on the basic goodness and morality of law-abiding citizens. Otherwise, this new experiment called the United States of America would have failed.

Perhaps this serves as a lesson for us today: No amount of legislation can solve our problems if basic human dignity, decency, and respect are lacking. We can't legislate morality. It must already be embedded in our culture. President Reagan cautioned us that this democracy of ours is fragile and precious—and could be lost in a single generation if we aren't good keepers of the flame!

Stew and Perry cover these principles, and so many others, in their most engaging book. They weave moving stories of their classmates, whose mothers and fathers were members of the Greatest Generation and taught them time-honored values, together with the lessons of the great leaders of history.

Inspiring Leadership: Character and Ethics Matter is a timeless and wonderful book that you will want to keep on the shelf and refer to often. It explores the very same principles that I used in my long coaching career at UCLA, and more importantly, as a father and a husband. It's a great read!

Coach John Wooden
June 28, 2004

Introduction

"IT IS IMPORTANT THAT PEOPLE KNOW WHAT YOU STAND FOR. IT'S EQUALLY IMPORTANT THAT THEY KNOW WHAT YOU WON'T STAND FOR."

MARY WALDROP

Why another book on leadership, ethics, or character development? Why is it essential to read and understand how one's worldview ultimately affects strong ethical character and competent leadership? Where can leaders turn for guidance on ethical dilemmas? These thought-provoking questions motivated us to tackle this project head on.

This is a book about why character does matter. It is not just a basic checklist for ethical leadership, but is written as a guide for deep reflection. Although it is sometimes much easier for authors of leadership books to answer these questions with vague abstractions, we chose instead one simple premise: Doing the right thing is based on a leader's character.

Experts in the field of leadership and ethics too often preach that no solution is more correct than another, but this politically correct waffling does a great disservice to those seeking real answers. This risk-avoidance approach is dangerous and creates a moral compass spinning aimlessly. Rather than fall into this trap, we decided to focus on a microcosm of leaders who today influence nearly every aspect of life in our country. We surveyed many of our fellow Naval

Academy classmates who comprise this special fraternity and we are sincerely indebted to them for their careful and insightful reflections about leadership and their core values.

U.S. NAVAL ACADEMY CLASS OF 1971

The United States Naval Academy is located on the banks of the Severn River in Annapolis, Maryland. The central campus, affectionately known as "the Yard," is located three blocks from the Maryland State House, two blocks from the Annapolis City Dock, and is twenty-five miles south of Baltimore and thirty miles east of Washington, D.C. The main campus began as Fort Severn in 1808 and was converted to a military college known as the Naval Academy in 1845.[1] On June 28, 1967, 122 years later, 1,384 young men gathered for their first day together, culminating with induction as "plebes" into the United States Naval Academy Class of 1971. Housed together in Bancroft Hall, the world's largest single dormitory, these new midshipmen would spend the next four years together in quest of a commission in the Naval Service and a diploma from one of the nation's most respected and distinguished institutions.

There is little doubt that this group brought a shared value system with them to Annapolis on that sunny Induction Day in 1967. Nearly every single plebe in the Class of 1971 was a descendant of the Greatest Generation. Their lives were immersed in a worldview rooted in a value system established by their fathers, grandfathers, and uncles who fought in World War II. Moreover, those whose ancestors survived the cruelty of the Great Depression passed down a special appreciation of the hardships of life and the perseverance and courage required to overcome seemingly insurmountable obstacles. They had arrived in Annapolis from every corner of the nation and few were strangers to the core values of the Academy: honor, courage, and commitment. Ethical and moral behavior was *expected* and accountability for one's actions was certainly not a foreign concept to this new group of fledgling plebes.

Although not unique in their childhood experiences compared to their civilian counterparts, they were about to enter a four-year leadership laboratory and complete the critical requirements of the mission of the Naval Academy: "To develop midshipmen morally, mentally, and physically and to imbue upon them the highest ideals of duty, honor, and loyalty in order to provide graduates who are dedicated to a career of naval service, and have the potential for future development in mind and character to assume the highest responsibilities of command, citizenship, and government."[2]

On June 9, 1971, at the Navy-Marine Corps Memorial Stadium in Annapolis, 874 men graduated from the United States Naval Academy. As the decade of the '60s disappeared behind them, the clouds of war loomed ahead of them as the Vietnam conflict continued to rage in Southeast Asia. Few could have predicted that the war would virtually be over in a matter of months following graduation. During their four-year stay in Bancroft Hall, images of the war were frequently posted on "the Board" in the Rotunda where rows of graduation photos showed those held in captivity as prisoners of war, and those killed or missing in action. Many of the 1971 graduates realized that war was inevitable and that soon critical leadership decisions would truly test their value system and their character. They would reach the highest positions in their chosen careers in the military, then later in government, education, business, and a myriad of corporate organizations from coast to coast. Often they would be challenged to make ethical decisions based on their belief system.

Thirty-three years later, we asked several of our classmates from the Class of '71 to reflect on their experiences in those early years and how those experiences impacted their effectiveness as ethical leaders. In subsequent chapters, we will explore their thoughts and reflections.

At the heart of this book is a framework of deep reflections drawn from this primary source. Chapter after chapter contain the insights of these prominent men who are now proven leaders in private and public life. Many are also respected leaders in their local communities and serve those in need of a healthy physical, mental, and spiritual life. These men of Annapolis share a comradeship that can never be broken. We have attempted to capture the very essence of their character by soliciting their insights into what great leadership really means. Most importantly, we weave their stories into those of other great leaders to create a book that will support you in your leadership and character development.

We want our observations and comments about this special group of leaders to foster deep reflection. We hope our effort revitalizes the importance of character and gives new meaning to ethical leadership. We fervently hope that it also enriches your life, that of your family, your community, and your country.

We want our book to have life-changing impact. At the end of each chapter you will find a "Reflection and Discussion" section with questions designed to stimulate your thinking, and more important- ly, spur you to action. We suggest that you keep a journal as you read each chapter. Your efforts at deep introspection can make a dramatic difference in your life and will be of immeasurable value long after you place this book back on the shelf.

Ethical leadership is important not only in your own life but also with those you lead to their full potential as human beings. It crosses all boundaries, all communities, and all nations. The world hungers for principled leaders who can unite us and inspire us.

There is much extraordinary work to be done, now more than ever.

Stew Fisher
Perry Martini
April 20, 2004

Acknowledgments

In writing this book, we have been the beneficiaries of the loving, caring, and generous assistance, advice, support, and above all, encouragement of others. The very topics we chose for each chapter are a reflection of the types of people we admire, love, and hope to emulate. They were instrumental in the completion of this project.

No book emerges solely from the minds of the authors. We have spent long hours asking our many Naval Academy classmates and friends for their reflections on what made them good leaders and how following the examples of others has made a difference in their lives. We are most grateful for their sincere contributions and opinions, for without their assistance, this book would not have come to fruition.

At "Boat School," if it hadn't been for roommates such as Ron Spratt, Mike DelBalzo, Garry Holmstrom, and Bruce Gallemore, or the "dirty dozen" of old Tiger 29, we doubt if we would have maintained our sanity or survived our four years at the Naval Academy, especially plebe year. There were times when we laughed so hard we could hardly breathe. We truly had our own "band of brothers."

We also owe a debt of gratitude to all those who have reviewed our work and provided sage advice, and especially those renowned authors who graciously wrote the testimonials that appear on the back of our book.

We certainly can't overlook the great men and women of history. As young boys, we devoured their biographies to learn their secrets. It made us realize the impact a person can have even when he or she lives in a different era. Even without meeting them, they can still inspire you. Of course, Jesus Christ has to be the one leader who most inspired us deeply and personally. Next would be Abraham Lincoln. Men and women of character have truly made a difference in our lives.

We always admired UCLA Coach John Wooden for his strength of character and strong leadership. We discovered that we admired many of the same leaders who had taught us enduring lessons in life. Coach Wooden, during a personal conversation, alluded to many of the same leaders we quoted in this book: the Good Lord, Abraham Lincoln, Mother Teresa, and Knute Rockne. Coach Wooden graciously agreed to write the foreword for our book and for that we are eternally grateful.

John Donne was so right when he said, "No man is an island." We are all touched by many people in our lives. Our only fear is that we might leave someone out who truly deserves to be mentioned. First, special thanks are in order for our families who have endured our long, isolated absences during countless hours of writing. In particular, my wife and best friend, Jean Martini, who truly displayed the patience of Job during my disappearances to the "writing room." Jean has always supported my endeavors 100 percent in spite of my attempts to juggle many balls simultaneously. Chapter 15, "Love and Friendship," speaks volumes on why I always depend on her wise counsel.

It should come as no surprise that I thank Audrey and Robert Fisher, my mom and dad, and Dr. John Fisher and Marian Kunz, my brother and sister, for their love and encouragement over all these years. My mom was an "Irish tiger" when it came to defending her kids. My Godmother, Aunt Ruth Macdonald, always kept me going with her words of encouragement. She's still an inspiration to me today. My uncle, Ben Ashcraft, was a great role model. Whenever he would see me beating myself up over some mistake I had made, he would simply ask, "Well, did you learn something?" He made me realize that was all that really mattered in life: learning from our mistakes and moving on. My cousins, Phil and Tinki Kilkeary, provided a welcome "port in a storm" during my days at Annapolis. I also benefited from my grandparents' wisdom, and spent many hours listening to them over cups of coffee. Later, when my granddad died, Norm Johanning filled that role and mentored me over many summers on Grand Traverse Bay in northern Michigan. I tagged along with him so much that he nicknamed me "Friday." Last, but certainly not least, I was blessed with four wonderful children, now in their 20s: Molly, Kelly, Patrick, and John Fisher. They made me want to become a better man so that I could be a better father. I never quite made it, but I'm still trying.

Part I
Character and Ethics:
They Do Matter

Chapter 1
Ethics

"WATCH YOUR THOUGHTS, FOR THEY BECOME YOUR WORDS;

WATCH YOUR WORDS, FOR THEY BECOME YOUR ACTIONS;

WATCH YOUR ACTIONS, FOR THEY BECOME YOUR HABITS;

WATCH YOUR HABITS, FOR THEY BECOME YOUR CHARACTER;

WATCH YOUR CHARACTER, FOR IT BECOMES YOUR DESTINY."

FRANK OUTLAW

Character and ethics *do* matter. We wanted our book to begin and end with this simple premise. Human beings are made in the image and likeness of the Creator as a permanent fusion of body, mind, and spirit. Like layers of an onion, our core is formed at birth, and then the foundation of our lives is progressively added throughout our development, best described as the reality of a worldview. For all humans, moral values are formed based on the environment and shared belief system of this worldview. All actions are shaped, to some degree, by both one's worldview and moral values. Worldview is a term introduced in the latter part of the twentieth century. It is essential that we establish a definition that explains why it is the core of one's reality.

WORLDVIEW

A worldview is the beliefs, ideologies, or stocks of knowledge that are held by people in a particular culture and socio-historical location. Worldview is the lens that people use to interpret their reality and assign meaning to events, experiences, and relationships in their world. Like DNA, it is unique to every person. The moral values that stem from our worldview guide all of our actions.

The concept of worldview is very broad. It refers to a person's overall perspective, including their belief about human nature, society, and the nature of the world around them, the meaning of life, or for that matter, belief in God. These beliefs affect behavior in many ways—both individually and collectively. For most, worldview is formed at the very core, the way people understand just who they are and their relation to the world around them.

Most historians would agree that the demise of the Soviet Union did not occur overnight, but rather as a total shift in worldview based on years of social and economical changes affecting millions of lives. It was a transition in worldview from socialism to capitalism. The Berlin Wall did not collapse in a single day or at the hands of a small group of individuals; it was the climax of a change in a belief system.

A belief system is what one accepts as truth. Values are based on one's beliefs and as we attach meaning to our values we truly can interpret the way we live. More importantly, this is how we establish the behavior pattern we use for our daily decisions. We think based on values, beliefs, and our worldview. Character is deeply rooted, expressed in our outward behavior.

CHARACTER

Character can be defined in a variety of ways. Perhaps the best definition is simply *the motivation to do what it is right; or who you are when no one is watching.* To be ethical, one must possess certain character qualities. Most of them actually originate in the Bible, such as patience, love, perseverance, self-control, humility, diligence, and so on.

Personal character influences behavior in a most dramatic manner. We can almost always trace back from behavior to find the meaning, values, and beliefs rooted in a person's worldview. The way we act has meaning based on what we believe about other people, the world, God, and ourselves. Love, perseverance, humility, integrity, and countless other character qualities have permeated all societies throughout history. However, whenever worldviews undergo rapid change due to technological advancement, economical change, or social revolution, one's corresponding value system, and ultimately one's character, are challenged and affected—sometimes dramatically.

VALUES

Much was written about values in the United States in the 1950s. Post World War II technological advancements were clearly apparent on the American scene with the dawn of the television age, the transistor radio, commercial jet travel, and many more. In spite of Cold War fears, the American society experienced the glow of peace and prosperity and a resurgence of traditional religious values. At the end of the decade, the United States and the Soviet Union entered the space age and the world experienced a quantum leap in communications capability with satellites orbiting the planet. The 1960s brought new challenges to this peaceful society. The United States was beginning to move dramatically from a religious to a non-religious worldview. Many "traditional" values relating to familiar obligations, human sexuality, work ethic, and other morals and practices were changing rapidly.

Institutions of higher learning flourished in this post-war era as many veterans took advantage of education benefits and returned to college to receive degrees. Moreover, families greatly increased in size due to the Baby Boomer generation, those born between 1946 and 1964, and higher education experienced a significant increase in applications for entrance in the mid-1960s.[1] The United States was deeply involved in a politically complex conflict in Southeast Asia, and the military draft was starting to have a great impact on young men graduating from high school. Increasing numbers were called to active duty in order to meet the demands of the expanding war effort. Not surprisingly, these events increased college applications for those seeking a deferment from the draft. At the same time, there was a dramatic increase in applications to the service academies.

4

ETHICS

Character's relationship to ethics is based on how we behave in situations we confront on a daily basis. Being ethical means doing the "right thing." Ethical behavior is linked to one's moral values. While there can be many kinds of values—such as aesthetical, political, and economical ones—the values we are focusing on in this book are ethical or moral ones. Everyone, regardless of ethical orientation, has moral values. No one has been developed in a moral vacuum. Most people can trace the formulation of their values to religion, family, culture, and personal experiences, through either a conscious or subconscious rejection or acceptance of values that have been learned. These values are a part of our everyday actions and behavior. They are manifested when we say what we believe and then do it.

Whether we like it or not, all of us are constantly making decisions that are shaped by our ethical values. No matter who we are, there is no escape from making decisions on issues that are essentially moral in character. Therefore, we are also ethical decision-makers, and when it comes to leadership, character and ethics matter.

Ethical decision-making can be both a skill and an art. It is a skill because analytical tools greatly enhance our ability to be competent, ethical decision-makers. However, just knowing the tools of ethical analysis does not make us proficient in ethical decision-making. Good ethical decision-making is also an art. It requires an intuitive ability to examine a highly complex ethical situation and focus on the heart of the matter. Undeniably, effective ethical decision-making requires that indefinable quality we usually refer to as character.

Character in this context is the courage and conviction to make difficult and unpopular decisions. Decision-making is inherent in leadership. One must often face a challenge in choosing the right course of action. Often this dilemma involves being ethical. But what makes a person ethical? Is it correct knowledge about right and wrong, good and evil that makes one ethical? Right or correct knowledge will not ensure that I act consistently with what is good. What makes someone ethical is the *practice* of ethical behavior. Our actions cannot be separated from our motives and intentions. Furthermore, our character is reflected in our behavior. Indeed, we are what we do. Therefore, ethics attempts to harmonize right thinking (intentions) with right behavior (action). In our human nature we are often morally weak, and even knowing the right thing will not guarantee that we will choose the right course of action.

Leadership becomes inspirational when difficult decisions are made with absolute moral conviction. The question that often plagues humans is "Why should I be ethical?" Ethical principles, laws, and moral criteria become meaningless and have no impact if they are not acted upon. Leaders, in spite of their frailties, biases, and limitations, still have the ultimate power to act and decide. Character means having the courage to make difficult and unpopular decisions.

Character *does* matter.

REFLECTION AND DISCUSSION

1. Write down your own definition of character and ethics.

2. List those values that are most important in your life.

3. In your opinion, why do character and ethics matter for leadership to be effective?

4. Can you describe your worldview and how it affects your overall behavior?

Chapter 2
Integrity

"IT WAS CLEAR TO ME THAT THE NAVAL ACADEMY BELIEVED IT WAS
IMPORTANT FOR ONE TO POSSESS INTEGRITY. AT THE END OF MY PLEBE
YEAR, I KNEW I MADE THE RIGHT DECISION ON BEING A MIDSHIPMAN."

VADM JIM METZGER, USN
ASSISTANT TO THE CHAIRMAN
JOINT CHIEFS OF STAFF
JULY 22, 2003

Most dictionaries list more than twenty individual definitions of the word "character." It is curious to note that few, if any, list the primary descriptor as a "moral or ethical quality." In the context of leadership, character can be easily defined as the courage to make difficult and sometimes unpopular decisions. Moreover, the recognized dictionary definition of the word "integrity"—adherence to moral and ethical principles, soundness of moral character; honesty; virtue[1]—gives little doubt as to the meaning of such an important word in the English language. While conducting a survey of the members of the United States Naval Academy Class of 1971, we asked them what values they considered most important to them as leaders. The number one value declared by nearly every respondent was integrity, for it embodied the essence of sound moral character necessary to be a true leader.

It was clear upon reflection that integrity more often than any other leadership characteristic emerged as the single most important element in the leader-follower relationship.

The college students at the Naval Academy, unlike a civilian university, spend four years in a military leadership structure. The members of the senior class are selected for various positions of leadership ranging from a squad of freshmen, sophomore, junior, and senior midshipmen (about twelve), to the highest position as leader of the entire student body, commonly called the Brigade of Midshipmen. To be selected as the Brigade Commander at the Naval Academy has very little in common with being the president of the class at a college or university. There is no popular vote taken among one's peers but rather the naval officers at the Academy choose one individual to be the senior year leader. Midshipman Mike Hecomovich was chosen in 1971 to lead his class and the Brigade at Annapolis.

Mike's reflections of his days as the Brigade Commander are affectionately remembered as "defining moments as a future leader." Currently President and CEO of Global Marketing Services (GMS), he recalls the many occasions he was called upon to clarify his values, and that integrity was undoubtedly the essential element required for making difficult decisions. "It was overwhelming at times to be the final vote on an aptitude or honor board at the Academy," Mike recalled, "and I will never forget the final vote I was required to cast on a dear friend and classmate who was 'claiming' to be a conscientious objector merely days prior to graduation." As Brigade Commander, Mike's final and deciding vote was to expel his classmate. His integrity to do the right thing was never questioned by his peers or his superiors.

Mike makes it clear that if people are to willingly follow someone—whether it be into battle or the boardroom, the front office or the front lines—they want to be certain that the person is worthy of their trust and has integrity. They want to know that the person is truthful, ethical, and of sound moral character. The value system used to make a decision in 1971 may seem irrelevant in today's world, but it illustrates the importance of the development of one's worldview and belief system. When people talk about the qualities they admire in leaders, they often use "honesty" and "character" as synonymous with integrity. No matter what the setting, everyone wants to be fully confident in their leaders. To be fully confident, they have to believe their leaders are people of strong character and solid integrity. We want a leader who knows right from wrong and is willing to make a decision regardless of the unpopular fallout.

Mike Kehoe, another recognized leader during his days as a midshipman with the Class of 1971, spent nearly thirty years on active duty as a naval officer. Twice in his career, he was assigned at-sea commands aboard the world's most sophisticated and capable nuclear submarines. He then spent his final years at his alma mater as the Character Development Officer. During his tour at Annapolis, Mike was directly involved with establishing what became known as Integrity Development Seminars (IDS)—a series of monthly workshops where midshipmen, faculty, and staff discuss the various aspects and characteristics of integrity and character development.

Today, retired Captain Mike Kehoe is the Commandant of Cadets at the Culver Military Academy. He reflects fondly of his days as a midshipman, then years later as a Commanding Officer, and finally, Director of Character Development at the Naval Academy during his twilight tour. He experienced several defining moments during his naval career, occasions that demanded character when making critical decisions. He recalled that, "Facing an ethical dilemma, I was forced to tell the whole truth, which worked for the common good every single time. I constantly learned that one's principles had to be centered on uncompromising integrity, and to always learn from yours and others' mistakes. The bottom line is getting the job done and being an effective leader by acting ethically. It's what integrity is all about."

John Condon, president of Federal Services and Touchstone Consulting, arrived in Annapolis in 1967 having served as an enlisted man in the United States Marine Corps. A proven leader as a midshipman, he entered the Surface Warfare community and was ultimately assigned to command a Navy warship. Upon retirement from the Navy, John joined a major electronics company in a position that placed him among the top twenty executives. "Within the first two weeks of my employment, I witnessed behavior by some of the most senior executives in this company that can be described only as unprofessional and unethical," John recalled. "I realized, regardless of the generous compensation package offered to me by this Fortune 100 Company, that unless I resigned, I would be jeopardizing my personal integrity and reputation, which I valued much more than the financial rewards I would be enjoying." John made an important decision to take the high road and go with his gut instinct. He never wavered from what he learned as a young Marine, midshipman, and naval officer about leadership and character. Integrity can be demonstrated only by unwavering adherence to moral and ethical principles—whatever the cost may be.

Jim Metzger remained in the United States Navy long after his four-year journey at the Naval Academy. Currently a three-star Admiral, he has risen to command nuclear submarines, combat battle groups, and an entire fleet in the Western Pacific. As of this writing, he is the primary assistant to the Chairman of the Joint Chiefs of Staff, an esteemed position that will certainly lead to a future four-star assignment. Jim is a proven leader who has never forgotten his days at the Naval Academy, a place he holds dear to his heart, and gives credit to the lessons he learned there. He recalls an incident that occurred at the end of his plebe (freshman) year that has stayed with him for over thirty-six years. An upperclassman had posed a rather probing question about the temptation to break the rules on liberty when he discovered that Jim's hometown was less than thirty miles from Annapolis. He asked Jim, "Have you ever slipped out past curfew to visit your friends and family that live so close by?" At the time he perceived it as an attempt to trap him into lying to avoid being punished for breaking Academy regulations. Jim remembers pondering his statement and deciding, on the spot, that it would be far better to tell the truth, answer "Yes" and take his lumps rather than to lie and compromise his integrity. The senior midshipman applauded him for his integrity and honesty. "It was clear to me that the institution believed it was important for one to possess integrity," Jim recalled. "At the end of my plebe year, I knew I had made the right decision to become a midshipman at the Naval Academy."

While in the Pentagon serving among the highest leaders in the U.S. military, Jim Metzger spoke eloquently of how proud he was to be a product of the '50s and '60s and the fundamental values that permeated our country following World War II. As someone descended from the Greatest Generation, there was a total absence of equivocation and a renewed dedication to serve out his remaining years inspired by a worldview of life in a free country. Unquestionably, character and ethics matter to Jim.

We return to the now recognizable dictionary definition of integrity as "the adherence to moral and ethical principles, soundness of moral character; honesty; virtue."[2] The late Admiral Arleigh

Burke, Chief of Naval Operations in the late 1950s and early 1960s, wrote a short treatise on integrity that appeared in an October 1985 issue of *Proceedings*. While addressing dictionary definitions of integrity, Admiral Burke quoted from a plaque that had been hanging in an office of a colleague. It bears repeating and is quoted in its entirety:

"Integrity"

First you find yourself overlooking small infractions.

Soon you are participants in those infractions.

All too soon you find yourself trapped. You find out you

no longer can stand on a favorite principle.

Finding no way out, you begin to rationalize, and then

you are hooked.

The important fact that becomes clear is that those who travel

this path have misused the very basic quality expected of

a true professional.

They have compromised their integrity.[3]

Individuals are responsible for their own integrity. Many people and events will influence them, but, in the end, integrity is of their own making. People are responsible for establishing their own standards, and their choices determine the kind of actions they take in life. Ultimately, that defines their character.

Cal Thomas, a nationally syndicated columnist and media commentator, speaks unambiguously of integrity in his book,

The Wit and Wisdom of Cal Thomas: "A person's character and integrity is produced by his level of virtue, and this is reflected in the ethics by which he lives."[4] The last thirty years of the twentieth century have been three decades of inattention to character, virtue, morality, and compromise in the definition of right and wrong. The Baby Boomer generation is finally in a position to make policy and decisions that affect our great country. And we are realizing there are truths about integrity that cannot be ignored. We also recognize that we are products of those who grew up in a much less secular society in America in the 1950s and 1960s. The world may have changed in fifty years, but standards such as integrity and virtue are timeless.

REFLECTION AND DISCUSSION

1. Since no two people have the same values, how does a person acquire integrity or a set of standards by which to live?

2. Integrity, or lack of it, is not always discernible. Many people deceptively appear to have great integrity. How do you guard against being fooled by those superficial appearances?

3. Be wary of self-proclaimed virtue. If someone had personal integrity, then they wouldn't need to use press releases and public pronouncements to convince others of their worth. Agree or disagree?

Chapter 3
Truth

"I was born for this, I came into the world for this: to bear witness to the truth; and all who are on the side of truth listen to my voice. 'Truth?' said Pilate, 'What is that?'"

John 18:37

"O what a tangled web we weave, when first we practice to deceive!"

Sir Walter Scott

"A Midshipman will not lie, cheat, or steal."

Honor Concept
United States Naval Academy

"This above all else: To thine own self be true, and it follows as the night the day, that thou canst not then be false to any man."

William Shakespeare, Hamlet

"Truth"—no principle is more daunting, yet it becomes the central focus of the intellect. From mankind's first reflections about the world, the questions of what truth is, and whether we can attain it, have loomed large. Every philosopher has had to grapple with these questions. Every religion seeks to answer them. To define one's integrity is to measure the veracity of their behavior. Is what they say and do their true intent?

Since the early 1950s, the Naval Academy Honor Concept has been the standard of accountability for midshipmen. The Academy had adopted a traditional and informal method of dealing with honor violations in its first century of existence. However, midshipmen themselves created an Honor Concept, not an Honor Code, with the principle that midshipmen "will not lie, cheat, steal, or tolerate anyone who does." Since its inception, the Academy's emphasis was on using the Honor Concept as a means of inspiring the highest moral standards among members of the Brigade because the midshipmen themselves oversee the Concept's implementation.

Two midshipmen in 1951 were very much involved in the formulation of the Concept. The first was the Brigade Commander for the class of '51, William Lawrence. He would later become one of the longer held prisoners of war during the Vietnam conflict and eventually the Superintendent of the Naval Academy before he retired as a three-star Admiral. The second was from the class of '53, H. Ross Perot, who arguably has become one of the most successful business leaders among Naval Academy graduates.[1] The deeply held convictions regarding truthfulness were evident in their advocacy for an Honor Concept in 1950 and were clearly demonstrated in the decades to come. The first principle, which hasn't changed for over fifty years, insists that midshipmen maintain the highest standards of personal integrity. The Concept remains simple, yet its spirit is broad and covers all facets of a midshipman's life. Moreover, it forms the link to the high standards demanded of naval officers in a life of service. Without a doubt, honor, personal integrity, and loyalty to service are fundamental characteristics essential to any successful profession. The underlying power of the Concept is telling the truth and "doing what is right," as opposed to simply not breaking the rules.

Dub Hay arrived in Annapolis from a small town in Georgia the summer of 1967 with aspirations to become a Navy jet pilot upon graduation. The family values and belief system he brought to the Naval Academy were not unlike those he became exposed to as a young midshipman. Dub fulfilled his dream as a naval aviator and jet pilot. But with the end of the Vietnam conflict and his desire to pursue other interests, he entered the business world and rose to become Vice President of Nestle USA. Today he is a Senior Vice President of Starbucks Coffee. Early in his business career, a supplier tried to tempt Dub to compromise his Honor Concept. He promised Dub that he could become wealthy overnight if he would just guarantee a favored contract exclusively to that supplier, a proposal that basically amounted to a "kickback." Dub realized that honesty was paramount in business, and he was not about to turn his back on the values he learned growing up in Georgia and during his four years at the Academy. "Honesty is most important in business," according to Dub, "for without it, a company is doomed to fail."

It was once said that a single lie destroys a whole reputation of integrity. This is precisely the lesson Jim Metzger showed us in the previous chapter regarding integrity. He chose to tell the truth and risk spending a few weekends in detention at the Academy rather than compromise his integrity by lying. Unquestionably, dilemmas dealing with telling the truth are occasionally muddied by distortions of moral reasoning. Decision-making can be difficult if moral relativism enters the thought process. In our fear of playing the blame game, we rationalize that holding people accountable is no longer necessary. Our "no fault" society has led to no fault insurance, no fault divorce, and no fault extremism. It's as if you have to tell the truth only when it has no bearing on how it affects others or is insignificant in the outcome.

Mike Hecomovich recalls the honor boards he chaired as the senior ranking midshipman in 1971. The offenses of lying, cheating, and stealing were intolerable in the Brigade, and in many cases were cause for separation from the Naval Academy and banishment from the confines of Bancroft Hall. Mike knew the awesome responsibility he had been given as the chosen leader of his class. There were times when standing tall for what is right took courage when issues of truth were pitted against classmate loyalty. Again, integrity takes priority over competing obligations or loyalties.

Jim Bryant graduated with the class of 1971 and spent more than twenty-three years as a naval officer. His career was highlighted by command of a nuclear submarine. Jim recalled the many lessons he learned regarding honor while attending the Academy. When faced with an honor issue as a young plebe, he realized the importance of thinking while under pressure and understood that decisions made, even under stress, have to hold up to scrutiny. Jim recalled, "There was a distinct difference in the Honor Concept at the Naval Academy and what West Point called the Honor Code. Moreover, the concept allowed us to inform and counsel an individual on wrongdoing and to ensure that the individual was fully aware of his mistake and to 'turn himself in' to the upper class to clear the air so to speak."

Jim Bryant is now the president and CEO of a major Washington, D.C. metropolitan cab company and rarely faces a day without dealing with insurance fraud, attempts by others to steal from his company, or some kind of deception to avoid payment. Jim concluded that, "Every time I face a possible ethical dilemma having to do with deception, I make myself think it through several times to make sure my decision is not being rationalized unethically."

Bruce Nichols is co-chairman of the California State University San Marcos Trust Board and the chairman of the California State University San Marcos College of Business Advisory Board. A graduate of the Class of 1971, Bruce spent six years in the surface Navy before becoming a civilian and entering the business world. He quickly turned hard work into profit and became chairman and president of a multibillion-dollar manufacturing industry and spent five years as Chairman and CEO of Formulabs, Inc. Bruce learned of his sudden rise to the chairmanship of Formulabs, Inc. when he was stunned by the news that his business partner had died unexpectedly from a massive heart attack. "I never looked back, for in that instant I was a changed person," Bruce recalled. "I had trained all of my life as far back as my Academy days to be a leader and to assume command. More importantly, my value system made integrity my primary motivation. It required unquestioned honesty and ethical behavior for me to succeed."

Retired Marine Colonel Bob Cabana, currently Director of Flight Crew Operations at NASA, is one of four members of the Naval Academy Class of 1971 who became astronauts. No other service academy class can boast of this many members of their class becoming space travelers, and Colonel Cabana distinguished himself by becoming the NASA Director of the Joint Human Space Flight Program with Russia following command of two space shuttle missions. His value system has never wavered since his Academy days, and he has directly applied the policy of total honesty in "dealing with people who work for me and for those I worked for." He further stated, "Having total honesty in dealing with the resources of an organization has always ensured that we operate with the utmost integrity and professionalism." Telling the truth is without boundaries, for it applies to the earthbound as well as to those who travel into the great frontier of space.

To be honest is to be real, genuine, authentic, and bona fide. To be dishonest is to be forged or fake. Honesty imbues lives with openness, reliability, and candor; it expresses a disposition to live in the light. Dishonesty fails to respect oneself or others. Furthermore, it seeks cover or concealment. Dishonesty is a disposition to live in shade or in darkness. Honesty is critical to all of our interactions. Most of us remember from our stories and legends the bedrock honesty of Abraham Lincoln, our sixteenth President. On the other end of the spectrum, we remember the lengthening nose of the oft-dishonest Pinocchio, thanks to the classic nineteenth-century Italian tale.

Americans, for the most part, do not take kindly to public figures or national celebrities being less than honest. Even the most avid baseball fan will continue to have a problem with baseball great, Pete Rose, who lied repeatedly about his gambling habits as a player and a manager. Worse yet, he committed the unforgiving act of lying about the lie for nearly fifteen years until it was too late to be sincerely contrite. Presidents, members of Congress, judges, policemen, teachers, and other public figures are held to the highest standard of honesty. We hold them more accountable for their actions because we expect them to be innately truthful, credible, and worthy of our trust.

Research conducted in the late 1990s has continued to affirm that Abraham Lincoln and Martin Luther King, Jr. were our most admired inspirational leaders for, above all, their honesty and forthrightness.[2] Although these two leaders lived a century apart, in times of national struggle, they always demonstrated unwavering commitment to the truth. Leaders like Abraham Lincoln and Martin Luther King, Jr. are inspirational because they give us moral clarity. We admire and respect honest leaders who courageously stand for something.

Truth is the linchpin for the Naval Academy virtues of honor, courage, and commitment. All midshipmen understand that truth cannot be compromised. They know that naval officers must exhibit the highest standards of honesty and integrity. This sets the bar high. Those who enter the leadership-learning lab at Annapolis know full well that their belief systems will be quickly measured against those values dependent upon truth: honor, courage, and commitment.

REFLECTION AND DISCUSSION

1. Do you consider honesty to be your most esteemed value? If not, what value is most important to you?

2. Have you ever seen lying determine the course of a person's professional life? How has it affected your profession?

3. Which public figures do you believe are truthful? How did they demonstrate their honesty?

4. Is it possible for a leader to be effective without being completely forthright?

Chapter 4
Honor, Courage, and Commitment

"I would lay down my life for America, but I cannot trifle with my honor."

ADMIRAL JOHN PAUL JONES

"Courage is fear hanging on for one minute longer."

GEN. GEORGE S. PATTON

"Commitment is the test of a man's courage."

LORD ADMIRAL JOHN JERVIS

HONOR

Honor, Courage, and Commitment. From time in memoriam, these valued words have been the cornerstone of the United States Naval Academy. This phrase emblazons the cover of the Admissions Catalogue, and is always on the lips of the men and women who today comprise the 4,000+ Brigade of Midshipmen. The words are not taken lightly as the graduates receive their commissions and enter into multiyear-long commitments to serve their country as members of the United States Navy and United States Marine Corps.[1]

In the many wars fought since the doors of this honorable institution first opened in 1845, graduates of the Naval Academy have served with honor, courage, and a commitment to defend the freedoms we still enjoy today. Beginning with the Civil War, and continuing through the Spanish-American War, World War I, World War II, the Cold War, the Vietnam War, and the present War on Terror ("Enduring Freedom"), graduates of the Naval Academy willingly gave their lives to protect our country against all enemies.

As previously mentioned, the Honor Concept remains the bedrock of life at the Academy in spite of an atmosphere of political correctness in the country at large that seeks to undermine it. There is no doubt that to lie, cheat, or steal cannot be tolerated among those who serve together, and moral clarity must be maintained in times of peace and war.

Steve Ayers graduated with his Naval Academy class in 1971. Today he holds the distinguished position of Senior Vice President for Contracts, Procurement, and Ethics at Science Applications International Corporation (SAIC), a multibillion-dollar company that employs over forty-two thousand men and women worldwide. Following graduation, he served honorably as a naval officer aboard nuclear submarines and has never forgotten the lessons of his past. In his position as chairman of the ethics committee at SAIC he notes, "I firmly believe that real ethics is doing the right thing when no one knows about it. It's dealing with situations in an honorable way, telling the truth, and not compromising your guiding principles and beliefs. The Honor Concept at the Naval Academy taught me to have the courage to be a truly inspirational leader and to stand for things that really matter."

Honor is a virtue above all others. When faced with decisions that make us reflect on what we believe to be the truth, it becomes a true test of one's character. It takes moral courage to put the truth into action. C.S. Lewis wrote, "Courage is not simply one of the virtues but the form of every virtue at the testing point."[2]

COURAGE

General Patton used to say, "Courage is fear hanging on for one minute longer." Without fear there can be no courage. Without something to overcome, where would be the challenge?

A chief petty officer once said to me, "Sir, I don't feel I have courage because I have feelings of fear." I told him I disagreed. Courage is not the absence of fear; it is taking action in spite of your fear. People who act without feeling fear are merely foolhardy, but certainly not courageous.

The greatest courage is often not physical at all. It's psychological. We all want to be popular, to be liked, to belong. But frequently, taking a courageous stand requires doing something that isn't popular, but right.

Leaders sometimes encounter devil's advocates. They are a precious resource, worth their weight in gold. Cultivate them and listen to them. They are demonstrating true courage, often risking

31

their careers by speaking up and letting the emperor know that he doesn't have any clothes on—or at least is getting down to his underwear. They are rare indeed and are probably great natural leaders themselves. They have the qualities you want on your team. By the same token, beware of "yes men." They will try to stifle the devil's advocates and tell you what they think you want to hear. They're no help to you or your organization.

The fear of not being liked can tempt leaders to seek popularity in order to get respect. Ironically, just the opposite will happen: You will have neither popularity nor respect. Have the courage to do what is right first and respect will follow. False friends will wither away, but true friendships and popularity can be built only on a foundation of respect.

Show courage and be in the arena, as Teddy Roosevelt would say:

"It is not the critic who counts, not the man who points out how the strong man stumbled or where the doer of deeds could have done better. The credit belongs to the man who is actually in the arena; whose face is marred by dust and sweat and blood...and who at worst, if he fails, at least fails while doing greatly, so that his place will never be with those timid souls who know neither victory nor defeat."[3]

COLONEL JOSHUA L. CHAMBERLAIN

It was a desperate moment. The troops of the Twentieth Maine had been ordered to defend the left flank of the Union line at

Gettysburg "at all costs." Led by Colonel Joshua L. Chamberlain, a thirty-five-year-old college professor and Christian theologian, the men from Maine had successfully repulsed repeated attacks by courageous Confederates from Alabama. Finally, exhausted and low on ammunition, the valiant soldiers from Maine appeared near the breaking point. As the determined Southerners renewed the attack on Little Round Top with another assault against the Union left flank, Chamberlain knew what was at stake. If his troops could not hold the line and the flank was turned, the Union army might be destroyed, the battle lost—and the war with it.

Facing what appeared to be certain defeat, Chamberlain did the unexpected: He ordered a bayonet charge! The battle-weary men in blue obediently fixed bayonets, charged down the hill into the face of the enemy—and shattered the final Confederate assault. The day was won.

Chamberlain would rise to brigadier general, survive four battle wounds, officially receive the surrender of Lee's army at Appomattox, and enjoy postwar prominence as governor of Maine. Yet despite his many achievements he would always be remembered for his leadership in those desperate moments at Little Round Top on the second day at Gettysburg.

Like his Confederate counterpart, General Robert E. Lee, Chamberlain would be revered for his wartime character. How did he and his troops do it? He would be asked that question repeatedly for the rest of his life. His reply, "In the privations and sufferings endured in battle, some of the highest qualities of manhood are called forth: courage, self-command, and sacrifice of self for the sake of something held higher." To generations of Americans—Southerners as well as Northerners—Joshua Chamberlain would hold an enduring position as the "Hero of Little Round Top."[4]

LIEUTENANT COMMANDER BUTCH O'HARE

World War II produced many heroes. One such man was Lieutenant Commander Butch O'Hare. Upon his graduation from the Naval Academy in 1937, he received his Navy "Wings of Gold" after intensive training in Pensacola, Florida, and was subsequently assigned as a fighter pilot on the aircraft carrier USS *Lexington* in the South Pacific.

One day his entire squadron was sent on a mission. After he was airborne, he looked at his fuel gauge and realized that someone had forgotten to top off his fuel tank. Because he would not have enough fuel to complete his mission and get back to his ship, his flight leader told him to return to the carrier.

Reluctantly, Butch dropped out of formation and headed back to the fleet. As he was returning to the mother ship, he saw something that turned his blood cold. A squadron of Japanese Zeroes was speeding their way toward the American fleet. The American fighters were already gone on a sortie and the fleet was all but defenseless. He couldn't reach his squadron and bring them back in time to save the fleet; nor could he warn the fleet of the approaching danger.

There was only one thing to do. He must somehow divert them from the fleet. Laying aside all thoughts of personal safety, he dove into the formation of Japanese planes. Wing-mounted fifty calibers blazed as he charged in, attacking one surprised enemy plane and then another. Butch weaved in and out of the now broken formation and fired at as many planes as possible until finally all his ammunition was spent. Undaunted, he continued the assault. He dove at the planes, trying to at least clip off a wing or tail, in hopes of damaging as many enemy planes as possible and rendering them unfit to fly. He was desperate to do anything he could to keep them from reaching the American ships.

Finally, the exasperated Japanese squadron took off in another direction. Deeply relieved, Butch O'Hare and his tattered fighter limped back to the carrier. Upon arrival, he reported in and related the event surrounding his return. The film from the camera mounted on his plane told the tale. It showed the extent of Butch's daring attempt to protect his fleet. He had destroyed five enemy bombers.

That was on February 20, 1942, and for that action he became the Navy's first ace of World War II and the first naval aviator to win the Medal of Honor.

A year later he was killed in aerial combat at the age of twenty-nine. But his hometown would not allow the memory of that heroic action die. Today, O'Hare Airport in Chicago is named in tribute to the courage of this great man.

So the next time you're in O'Hare, visit his memorial with his statue and Medal of Honor. It is located between Terminals One and Two.

"EASY EDDIE"

Some years earlier there was a man in Chicago called "Easy Eddie." At that time, Al Capone virtually owned the city. Capone wasn't famous for anything heroic. His exploits were anything but praiseworthy. He was, however, notorious for enmeshing the city of Chicago in everything from booze and prostitution to murder.

Easy Eddie was Capone's lawyer and for a good reason. He was very good. In fact, his skill at legal maneuvering kept Big Al out of jail for a long time. To show his appreciation, Capone paid him very well. Not only was the money big; Eddie got special dividends. For instance, he and his family occupied a fenced-in mansion with live-in help and all of the conveniences of the day. The estate was so large that it filled an entire Chicago city block. Yes, Eddie lived the high life of the Chicago mob and gave little consideration to the atrocities that went on around him.

Eddie did have one soft spot, however. He had a son whom he loved dearly. Eddie saw to it that his young son had the best of everything: clothes, cars, and a good education. Nothing was withheld. Price was no object. And despite his involvement with organized crime, Eddie even tried to teach him right from wrong.

Yes, Eddie tried to teach his son to rise above his own sordid life. He wanted him to be a better man than he was. Yet, with all his wealth and influence, there were two things that Eddie couldn't give his son, two things that Eddie sacrificed to the Capone mob that he could not pass on to his beloved son: a good name and a good example.

One day, Easy Eddie reached a difficult decision. Offering his son a good name was far more important than all the riches he could lavish on him. He had to rectify all the wrong that he had done. He would go to the authorities and tell the truth about "Scarface" Al Capone. He would try to clean up his tarnished name and offer his son some semblance of integrity.

To do this he must testify against the Mob, and he knew that the cost would be great. But more than anything, he wanted to be an example to his son. He wanted to do his best to make restitution, and hopefully, have a good name to leave his son. So, he testified. Within the year, Easy Eddie's life ended in a blaze of gunfire on a lonely Chicago street. He had given his son the greatest gift he had to offer at the greatest price he would ever pay.

What do these two stories have to do with one another? Butch O'Hare was Easy Eddie's son.[5]

COURAGE TO ENTER THE LAST FRONTIER

What is courage? Does it take courage to strap into a spacecraft with a million pounds of liquid propellant to fuel its three main engines and two solid rocket motors with better than five and one-half million pounds of thrust? Does it take courage to stand on the roof of the Launch Control Center, next to the wife of your best friend and fellow astronaut, holding their two-year-old in your arms, while he and six other of your closest buddies rocket into space on top of a ball of flame? Or does it take courage to inform the families of one of your assigned crews that their loved ones will not be coming home again? Courage comes in many different forms.

The Naval Academy Class of 1971 has the distinct honor of having more graduates enter the space program than any other college, university, or service academy. Four members of '71 have entered the last of the great frontiers and have been an integral part of the country's space exploration program. When asked about courage, Colonel Bob Cabana, USMC, one of '71's four astronauts and a frequent flyer in outer space, stated, "I've been asked if I was ever afraid sitting in the space shuttle waiting to lift off into low Earth orbit. The truth is, I was not. I thought only of doing my job to the very best of my abilities to ensure that I contributed all that I could to ensure the success of our mission and the safety of the rest of the crew. I never felt particularly courageous. I had great faith in my training and the NASA team that prepared the shuttle, and in my God who would look after me and my family no matter how things turned out."

Undoubtedly, courage is being prepared whenever you're called upon to serve. Courage is being more concerned for the safety of your team than for yourself. Courage is having the moral conviction to stand up for what you believe in and doing your job to the best of your abilities regardless of your environment.

We show courage every day in little ways that help us learn about ourselves. Courage has been personified in the stories and reflections of Colonel Chamberlain, Lieutenant Commander Butch O'Hare, "Easy Eddie" O'Hare, and Colonel Bob Cabana. The practice of facing our worst fears with courage and bravery in the service of others becomes a deep well that we can draw upon. It ultimately becomes part of our character and allows us to be stead-fast in future times of peril.

COMMITMENT

And what of commitment? In Chapter Two we focused on integrity. Consider that integrity means to stay true to one's commitment, regardless of the circumstances. Making a commitment is something we do whenever we have the moral courage, and the willingness, to do what we feel is right in spite of the risk.[6]

Rear Admiral Joe Enright of the Class of 1971 made a lifetime commitment to service in the submarine community. He has served as a Carrier Group Commander as well as commanding the U.S. Navy submarine forces in the Western Pacific. When asked his thoughts on leadership, he offered this: "Making a commitment to not only trust your instincts but to trust your people is paramount with regards to great leadership. We need to be reminded often that we have made a commitment to take care of each other and to do the right thing."

Honor, Courage, and Commitment. Our own honor, our selfless courage, and our steadfast commitment to something higher than ourselves define us as leaders. They are the virtues we use to demonstrate our love of country and to serve her as true patriots.

REFLECTION AND DISCUSSION

1. What does honor mean to you? Is it a reflection of your belief system?

2. Do you agree that true courage cannot exist without fear being present also?

3. How would you compare physical and moral (psychological) courage? Which is more challenging?

3. Give examples of leaders who showed exceptional courage.

4. Must leaders demonstrate commitment in order to lead well?

5. Reflect on those leaders who demonstrated a lack of moral fiber because they failed to make a commitment to their stated values.

Chapter 5
Patriotism

"I ONLY REGRET THAT I HAVE BUT ONE LIFE TO LOSE FOR MY COUNTRY."

NATHAN HALE

December 7, 1941, and September 11, 2001. Forever linked in infamy, the events that occurred on these two dates had an effect of apocalyptical magnitude on our blessed land. Pearl Harbor signaled the commencement of our entry into World War II, while "9/11" ushered in our counter-offensive in the War on Terror. We all wept at hearing the news that fateful morning in 2001. We all felt unabashed compassion and love for those who lost their lives. The utter shock and sadness we witnessed on national television created a bond with our fellow citizens on those doomed airliners, the people in the twin towers, and the men and women of the Pentagon, causing our patriot blood to boil.[1]

Franklin D. Roosevelt, our thirty-second President, called upon all Americans on December 8, 1941, to stand tall as America entered the Second World War in response to the attack on Pearl Harbor. George W. Bush, our forty-third President, displayed admirable character and resolve and told the grieving nation that we would be entering a War on Terror and not retreating until the enemy was defeated and eliminated. In both cases, patriotism ran high; flags fluttered on every street corner; voices were raised to the stirring hymns of "America the Beautiful" and "God Bless America."

Patriotism stirs the hearts and minds of all who remain loyal to the red, white, and blue, but the outburst of emotion can be short-lived. In times of crisis, as in the aftermath of 9/11, do we as Americans possess the ideological integrity and patriotic stamina required for the long haul? Or is our patriotism only lukewarm? Worse yet, have we been known to publicly denigrate the concept of patriotism in order to remain politically correct? In the end, heroes emerge who stand tall for our country. Thankfully, we never seem to run out of Americans who possess character and are willing to die, if necessary, to preserve our liberty and freedom.

Character, thoroughly defined in Chapter One, is not just formed by academic instruction in the moral virtues. When we see real heroes in action, they inspire us to emulate their lives. Their example stirs our deepest hopes and aspirations.

We find a thirst for heroes in every culture. But a society that misguidedly worships celebrities, that allows the end to justify the means, or that feeds on resentment and rage will produce the wrong kinds of heroes and citizens with the wrong kind of character. Sadly, in America, too, we've sometimes chosen poor role models. In the Middle East, it's Osama Bin Laden or Yasser Arafat. They are celebrated, they are "great names," but none are great men.

But America, by the grace of God, can still produce great men and women. Since 9/11 and the War on Terror, we've been reminded of that daily. Ask a young boy what he wants to do when he grows up and he'll likely tell you he wants to be a fireman, an airline pilot, an astronaut, or serve in the military. Why is this so prevalent? What's in his heart that draws him to these professions? Simply, in them he finds heroes who make a difference and who are true patriots.

Heroes live with moral courage. They find the strength to do the right thing in the face of temptation and danger. They spend their lives helping and protecting others. That's what the human heart longs for, and even a little boy can understand something about sacrifice and goodness.

SEPTEMBER 11, 2001

Two lives merged following a thirty-year separation on that fateful September morning in 2001. They were not only fellow Naval Academy graduates from the Class of 1971, but also played as fellow musicians in the Naval Academy Drum and Bugle Corps. Charles "Chic" Burlingame, a retired Navy captain, was the chief pilot of American Flight #77 on September 11, 2001. Departing from Washington Dulles Airport for an eventual destination of Los Angeles, a monstrous act of terror caused the flight to be terminated on the south side of the Pentagon in an horrific ball of flame. Ironically, while mayhem struck our nation, his fellow classmate and friend, Captain Frank Culbertson, USN, was the pilot in command of the Space Station, orbiting high above the Earth.[2]

Frank Culbertson was in a unique position in history. Not only did he have a bird's eye view of America being attacked in Pennsylvania, New York City, and Washington, D.C., he was the only American not on the planet that fateful day. Aboard the International Space Station, he wrote a poignant, personal letter to his Naval Academy class on September 11th and 12th, sharing his thoughts about what had transpired before his very eyes.

"As the news of occurring events was being passed to me from Houston, we were literally on the other side of the world. The news seemed surreal. I was flabbergasted, then horrified. I glanced at the world map on the computer and knew we would be passing over New England in a few minutes. I zipped across the station until I found a window that would give me a view of New York City and Washington, D.C., and grabbed the nearest camera. As I looked down, we witnessed the collapse of the second Twin Tower. The smoke seemed to have an odd bloom to it at the base of the column. I turned my gaze toward Washington, D.C. There was a haze of smoke, but no specific source could be seen. It all looked incredible from two to three hundred miles above the Earth. I couldn't even imagine the tragic scenes on the ground."

He continued, "In addition to the emotional impact of our country being attacked and thousands of our citizens being killed, I was overcome by the utter isolation. We were flying in an area of

limited communication and as the only American without access
to news, I was distraught. I knew so many people in Washington, so
many who travel to D.C. and New York City, so many pilot friends,
that I felt certain more bad news was to follow. Then it hit me like
a ton of bricks. I was informed that the captain of the American
Airlines jet that hit the Pentagon was Chic Burlingame, a classmate and good friend. I couldn't imagine what he must have gone
through. And now, only hours later, I am told that he rose far beyond the call of duty as a true hero in possibly preventing his plane
from being the one to attack the White House. Many have said that
we astronauts are the patriotic heroes of our land, but I beg to dif-
fer. Chic epitomizes what it means to be selfless and, if necessary,
give your life in defense of our freedom. He, like many others who
gave their lives earlier today, represent what patriotism means in
the United States of America."

He concluded, "It's horrible to see smoke pouring from wounds
in your own country from such a fantastic vantage point. The di-
chotomy of being in a spacecraft dedicated to improving life on
the Earth and watching life being destroyed by such willful, terrible
acts is jolting to the psyche, no matter who you are. And the knowledge that everything will be different from when we launched by
the time we land is a little disconcerting. I have confidence in our
country and in our leadership that we will do everything possible
to better defend her and our families, and to bring justice for what
has been done."[3]

Chic Burlingame was laid to rest on a dreary fall day in 2001 at Arlington National Cemetery. He was given full military honors and buried near his father who had also faithfully served his country. Rear Admiral Christopher Weaver, USN, Commandant of the Washington Naval District and a classmate from the Naval Academy Class of 1971, represented the United States Navy as the Officer-in-Charge of the Honor Guard and presented the American flag to his widow following the twenty-one-gun salute. Vice Admiral Tim Keating, USN, Commander Fifth Fleet, and a classmate from the Naval Academy Class of 1971, delivered a stirring eulogy applauding Chic's life as a true friend, classmate, and patriot. Captain Frank Culbertson sat in the International Space Station, and became the first spaceman to play taps in space. He played it in honor of Chic, his friend and fellow trumpet player from his Naval Academy days. Later he wrote, "Playing taps gave me a sense of connection with Chic. It was a terrible loss, but I'm sure Chic fought bravely to the end. And tears don't flow the same in space."

No one will ever forget that fateful September day or the spirited patriotism and love of country all of us felt. As we buried our dead and fondly paid tribute to their memories, the country resolved to win the War on Terror.

"ENDURING FREEDOM," THE WAR ON TERROR

As we mentioned in Chapter One, nearly every single plebe who arrived in Annapolis in June 1967 as a member of the Class of

1971 was a descendant of the Greatest Generation. Their lives were literally immersed in a worldview based on a value system established by their fathers, grandfathers, and uncles who fought in World War II. Moreover, those whose ancestors survived the cruelty of the Great Depression of the 1930s passed down a special appreciation for the hardships of life and the perseverance and courage needed to overcome seemingly insurmountable obstacles. They had arrived in Annapolis from every corner of the nation and few were strangers to the core values of the Academy: honor, courage, and commitment. Ethical and moral behavior was *expected*, and accountability for one's actions was not a foreign concept. Moreover, the blood of patriotism and love of country flowed in their veins as it had for their fathers before them.

Four individuals from the Class of 1971 rose to prominence in the United States Navy and Marine Corps in 2001. For the first time in U.S. Navy history, three members of the same Naval Academy class served as the deployed Fleet Commanders: Vice Admiral Tim Keating, Commander Fifth Fleet; Vice Admiral Scott Frye, Commander Sixth Fleet; and Vice Admiral Jim Metzger, Commander Seventh Fleet. Lieutenant General John Sattler was serving as a Commanding General of the First Marine Division and was deployed to the Middle East and Far East Theaters to serve in the U.S.-led Central Command.[4] All were in operational command during the global war on terror, "Enduring Freedom."[5]

Lieutenant General John Sattler was asked about his thoughts on leadership a week after 9/11. His passionate response was given without hesitation, "...young men and women will be looking to many of us to set the example as we soon enter a path to war that has no precedent from history to guide us. Nor does this conflict have demographic boundaries. We will need to be leaders that inspire others to follow, and more than anything, not ask anything of our troops that we wouldn't do first. We motivate others by serving them first as we lead them to battle against a hidden enemy."

Vice Admiral Tim Keating was embroiled in Enduring Freedom within weeks of 9/11 as Commander Naval Forces Central Command and Commander of the Fifth Fleet while deployed to the Indian Ocean and Arabian Sea. His reflections on leadership following his tour were made upon returning to the Pentagon as Director of the Joint Chiefs of Staff. He said, "Leaders are inspirational only if they maintain the highest level of integrity and courage in the face of the enemy. Being a servant leader is so important that you almost have to treat others as you would want them to treat your children: with dignity and respect and by setting an example of service."

Vice Admiral Jim Metzger served as Commander Seventh Fleet, the Western Pacific Naval Command for all naval forces. Following his direct involvement in Enduring Freedom, he returned to the Pentagon to assume the duties of Assistant Chairman of the Joint Chiefs of Staff. In his new Pentagon position, he has worked directly with the Secretary of State and former Chairman of the Joint Chiefs of Staff, retired General Colin Powell, and closely observed his leadership style. Jim said, "Colin Powell is the consummate leader and my number-one role model. Possessing tremendous experience in affairs that directly affect our national interest, he has never lost sight of being evenhanded and fair. He is an inspiration to me in how he includes everyone in a decision and continues to serve others who follow him in spite of his lofty position. I wouldn't want anyone else to be our nation's representative in world affairs while we continue to fight the War on Terror."

So why this love of country, this devotion to duty and to others? And just why do we fight? Are we too timid to admit that our country is something to be proud of, something to truly celebrate? To shrink from being patriotic demonstrates gross ignorance of why the United States of America exists today. Patriotism is the reason we hunt down those who endanger our land, our way of life, and our sacred liberty and freedom. An objective view of our history demonstrates our noble purpose: We have provided more freedom to more people than any other nation in the history of mankind; we have provided a greater degree of equality and justice, more prosperity, and spread it more widely, than any nation in history; our open, tolerant, prosperous, peaceable society is the marvel and envy of the ages.[6]

We as a patriotic nation have been the beacon of freedom and opportunity to people throughout the world since the day of our creation. America is the place where people run to when, in hope or hopelessness, they are running from someplace else. Leaders with character inspire others to follow them and to fight to the end in order to preserve and protect these precious rights. They always do what is right and fully understand that American patriotism is not just a slogan but also a way of life in these United States.

Character and ethics *do* matter to those who must lead us.

REFLECTION AND DISCUSSION

1. Stephen Decatur once said, "My country, right or wrong, but right or wrong, my country." Would you agree, or say that a true patriot should speak up when his beloved country has gone astray?

2. Have we chosen the "wrong heroes" in America?

3. Does true patriotism ever go out of style or become old-fashioned?

4. Has contemporary American culture undermined patriotism?

5. Name some true patriots, past and present.

6. What is the most likely source of the next generation of patriots?

Part II
Advanced Leadership:
Traits That Inspire Winning Teams

Chapter 6
Fidelity and Obedience

"FIDELITY IS UP AND OBEDIENCE IS DOWN ON MY BAYONET BELT

BUCKLE, SIR!"

MIDSHIPMEN'S "REEF POINTS"

In the very first week of plebe summer, brand new midshipmen learn to march. It is a rite of passage for every man and woman who enters the military and is no different at the Naval Academy.

Engraved conspicuously on the bayonet belt buckles of these raw midshipmen are two words: fidelity and obedience, one above the other. In those first harrowing days of plebe summer, when a new plebe is asked by an upperclassmen, "What's up?" he answers in a loud voice, "Sir, fidelity is up and obedience is down on my bayonet belt buckle!"

So why are those two words given such emphasis? Simply, to indelibly impress on these young men and women how critical fidelity and obedience are to a winning team and victory in battle.

FIDELITY

The United States Marine Corps has a long and proud history. Their motto is "Semper Fidelis," or "Always Faithful." Every Marine has this concept deeply embedded within his character and soul. In fact, when two Marines greet each other or part company they say, "Semper Fi." With those two words they are reminding each other of the secret to the Marine Corps' esprit de corps, in effect saying, "I will never break faith with you and am even willing to die for you, as you are for me." No wonder there is such a powerful bond between them—and all Marines!

Fidelity also implies honesty and truth. What you see is what you get. You are the genuine article, someone who can always be counted on. You are committed to the goals of the team, no matter what, and the team always comes before self. That's critical in the life and death situations Marines often face even when training for combat.

Dan Nelson, graduate of the Class of 1971 and currently vice president for government affairs, ExxonMobil, went into the Marine Corps following graduation. He has never forgotten the bond and the deep commitment to excellence that were instilled in every Marine from those first days at Quantico. "The Marine Corps was amazingly black and white," he proudly recalled. "The training, the team spirit developed in the crucible of battle, and the absolute loyalty we felt for one another were infectious. The Marine motto, 'Semper Fi,' says it all. We never faltered from our mission or our faithfulness to each other."

Chuck Boyer, president of Your Business Group (YBG) from the Class of '71, fellow Marine and Vietnam veteran added, "We learned from the start that no matter what the circumstances, you were committed to each other; and the lives and safety of the unit always came before self. Fidelity means the absolute truth and integrity of one's spirit. There is no more pure institution that believes in God, country, and the faithfulness to each other as human beings than the United States Marine Corps."

Tom O'Brien has accomplished something no other member of the Class of '71 has been able to do: He is the head football coach at Boston College and at the helm of a very successful NCAA Division 1A football program. He knows what it takes to win, and that even a team with star athletes will fail without the synergy of the entire unit. He too served as a Marine following graduation, later pursuing a career as a football coach after leaving the Corps. Tom reflected upon his first Marine training, "They taught us to turn *into* the machine-gun fire, instead of running away from it! Looking back on this seemingly suicidal approach to combat, it now is clear that the only chance you had of winning was to go down shooting into the face of the enemy; otherwise you would lose the battle with your back to the fight. I know what it means to win and the determination it takes to be successful. Our emphasis on fidelity and faithfulness forms that powerful bond found only on winning teams."

Faithfulness says you have integrity. Your principles are not mere words but guideposts you truly live by. Long before compact discs became the standard for music, we used to describe long playing records as having "high fidelity," or "hi fi." That meant the music on the record was as true to the original sound as was humanly possible. The same analogy could apply to great leaders: They are true to their guiding principles and consistently respond with "high fidelity" to those principles in any situation.

OBEDIENCE

Obedience involves many aspects of a person's character. It first requires humility, a willingness to subordinate our interests for the common good. We all want to be heard, to have our own ideas and opinions prevail. But obedience makes us recognize the ideas and authority of others. Without it, coherent action is impossible because everyone would be going in different directions. Furthermore, no one can ever become a great leader if he hasn't learned to follow first. Before we can *give* orders, we must be able to follow them. Later, when the time comes to be a leader, we will have a better insight into what it feels like to be on the receiving end of directives, and have greater empathy for those who must carry them out. Aristotle once said that in order to be a good commander, one must learn the lessons of obedience.

There comes a time in every leader's life when someone will attempt to make him compromise his principles. This is especially challenging when that person is senior to the leader. A member of the Class of '71 faced this very same dilemma during his squadron command tour. His boss, the Wing Commander, let it be known in not too subtle fashion, that it was very important that a certain individual in the squadron be ranked as the number one department head (in order to secure promotion to future command).

The "performance review" in the Navy, commonly termed a FITREP (Fitness Report of Officers), is to be conducted with the highest degree of honesty and integrity. Moreover, it is one of the single most important decisions made by a Commanding Officer regarding his subordinates, for it determines the direction of their future careers in the United States Navy.

This particular squadron Commanding Officer resisted the coercion of his boss and chose to vote his conscience. Instead of naming the Wing Commander's favorite, he selected another more deserving officer as his number one department head. While the decision to ignore the Wing Commander's unlawful order later cost this squadron commander a future promotion, he has the pride of knowing he did the right thing in spite of tremendous pressure. He never compromised his integrity. Obedience to this "order" would have been easy to execute, but the damage to this courageous squadron CO's soul and character would have been irreparable.

As the story of the brave squadron CO illustrates, obedience should never become "blind obedience." It must never involve disengaging your mind and your heart from your actions. When following orders, you must constantly examine the required actions for fidelity to your principles. Unlawful orders must never be carried out. The cowardly justification, "I was just following orders," has led to some of the most egregious "crimes against humanity" history has ever seen, such as Nazi Germany's extermination of the Jews and Vietnam's My Lai massacre.

Defying an unlawful order may be the most courageous thing you will ever do, but you'll be in good company. Consider Army helicopter pilot, Hugh Thompson, door gunner, Lawrence Colburn, and crew chief, Glenn Andreotta, who landed their helicopter between American troops rampaging through My Lai village and the local people, refusing to allow their fellow soldiers to continue their massacre of innocent Vietnamese civilians. Or consider the moral courage of Attorney General Elliot Richardson in refusing to fire Special Prosecutor Archibald Cox, in spite of a direct order from President Nixon, at the height of the Watergate scandal. These were brave actions by brave men.

Incidents such as the My Lai massacre underscore the importance of having character that is strong enough to resist the directives of authority figures, when such directives are immoral or unlawful. It is not far-fetched to equate this challenge with doing business in corporate cultures that place a high value on hierarchical authority and compliance. Resisting "groupthink" and the unethical use of power requires moral backbone.

Obedience often requires courage and the ability to face our worst fears. It may involve great personal risk. Indeed, it may be daunting, both physically and emotionally. We will always remember those gallant men at Gallipoli during World War I, leaving heartfelt letters and keepsakes behind for loved ones, before climbing out of the trenches to go "over the top" to almost certain death.

Even if it doesn't involve a life or death matter or a compromise of principle, followers owe it to their leaders to offer feedback whenever another method may work better than the one proposed. This is simply healthy dialogue, and good leaders should never take offense or let their egos get in the way of such suggestions.

At the same time, everyone on the team needs to understand when a delay could create problems and be ready to take immediate action, assuming no principles will be compromised. If there is already good morale on the team, everyone will recognize the difference. They will intuitively know when there is time for more dialogue, and time only for immediate action.

REFLECTION AND DISCUSSION

1. What is your personal definition of fidelity?

2. What examples in history stand out as your models of fidelity?

3. Would you agree or disagree with the statement, "Disobedience can be a virtue"?

4. "If you've never been a follower, you can never be a leader." Agree or disagree?

5. When it comes to fidelity and obedience, what are some of the signs that a team has high morale?

6. What would you do if your job literally depended on obeying an unethical order? Facing a legal dilemma is easier to deal with than shaded ethical issues. Take a moment to reflect on how you deal with these everyday decisions in your personal and professional life.

Chapter 7
Communication

"WHAT IS COMMUNICATED FROM THE HEART ALONE WILL WIN THE
HEARTS OF OTHERS TO YOUR OWN."

GEOTHE

In any organization, on any team, in any family, or in any inter-action between two people, communication is the key to success or failure. When a problem occurs, you can invariably trace it back to poor communication.

Communication will always exist. But communication isn't always positive. Bad communication has another name: rumor. Wherever good communication is lacking, rumors will fill the void. Human beings can't stand not knowing. Without good information, they will make something up.

What should leaders do with this knowledge? Simply this: Always have open and honest communications using every available means of getting the word out. Never hoard information as a means of retaining power and control. It will only backfire. For example, open up the books if that's what the employees want. Show them the company's bottom line. Let them actually see why you could afford only a 2 percent pay raise this year. And be sure that upper management shared the pain and didn't get more. Like the Chrysler Company of the 1980s, workers will go to great lengths to bail out the lifeboat if they know they're in a desperate situation and there is only one lifeboat.[1]

Leaders set the tone, create a winning environment, and guide the culture of the organization. This is one of their most important roles. How do they do it? By communicating. That's how they control the message, control meaning in the organization. Unless they communicate often and repeatedly, using every method available, the company's mission, vision, and guiding principles will inevitably be lost. There will be no unity of effort on the team, no battle plan.

Use all the means of communication available: speeches, company newsletters, e-mail, suggestion boxes, informal open meetings (called "Captain's Calls" in the Navy). Use whatever is available to get your message out—and not just once. Think of your voice as an echo, which will eventually die out unless you reinforce it repeatedly.

Don't be afraid to open yourself up to the tough questions either, even though they'll challenge you. Remember, there's nothing wrong with saying, "I don't know. I'll get back to you on that one." Just be sure that you do, or else the message that you send to everyone is that the boss lacks credibility. Recognize too the natural tendency to not open up to the boss. Show employees that you view their candor as constructive and that it will never result in retribution.

If you create an open and honest communication network where the boss is responsive to all questions, people will feel that they have ownership in "the team," and morale will soar.

LISTEN!

Public speaking courses abound, but how many of us have ever been to a listening course? There are very few. And yet, a good conversation requires both: a speaker and a listener who's paying attention.

Isn't it interesting that we were born with two ears, but one mouth? Maybe that should tell us something about the importance of listening versus speaking. But too often our conversations are dueling monologues. We don't even bother to listen as we wait impatiently for our own turn to speak and "enlighten."

Dr. Stephen Covey tells us, "Seek to understand, before being understood."[2] That's good advice. Listening adds to our store of knowledge; speaking does not. Listening also sends a powerful message to the person speaking: "I have respect for you and what you are saying." And if we set that example with our own empathetic listening, there's a good chance it will be reciprocated.

How well do you listen? Do you monopolize the conversation because you're the boss? Do you think you're the only one with good ideas? Are you missing good inputs because of your attitude?

As a leader, be the last to speak. That will prevent your opinion from biasing the discussion. More untainted views from others will be voiced that way. People are more likely to say what's on their minds rather than what they think the boss wants to hear. Give praise to anyone willing to offer a contrary opinion. They are showing courage and may be saying the exact thing that needs to be heard. Remember, yes men are of no value.

USE STORIES AND ANALOGIES TO COMMUNICATE

Our greatest communicators were storytellers. Abraham Lincoln was known as "the great yarn spinner." As he traveled from town to town, riding the law circuit, people would flock to the local taverns just to hear him tell his amusing, often hilarious stories. In the courtroom, Lincoln would often illustrate the point he wanted to make, to great effect, with an illuminating analogy or story, winning over the jury.

The Bible is filled with Jesus' parables, stories that illustrate important lessons. And we all grew up hearing "Aesop's Fables."

Never overlook this powerful way of communicating. It can put an idea into language people immediately understand. People relate to stories.

Do you use stories and analogies to communicate? Are you missing out on this powerful communication tool?

INTUITION

Any examination of communication must not overlook the critical value of a leader's own internal communication, intuition.

Intuition is sometimes called the sixth sense. If you've ever said to yourself, "I knew that was going to happen!" then you've experienced intuition. The source of our intuition seems inexplicable. We just get this sense deep in our bones, or a sensation that's often called a "gut feeling."

Perhaps our practical nature makes us discount intuition, since it seems unquantifiable, not lending itself to empirical, scientific study and measurement. But throughout most of human history, we never understood electricity. It took years to unlock its secrets. Perhaps the mystery of intuition may be unraveled in a similar way.

In the meantime, let's not underestimate its vital importance to us as leaders. We must recognize that many inputs in the real world are constantly being processed by the mind—itself a marvelous and mysterious organ!—at the subconscious, subliminal level.

For example, without even being aware of it, we are continuously making judgments about what other drivers are going to do on the freeway. Maybe it's the way they look in their side view mirrors before they change lanes, or their inattention while using a cell phone, or an overall sense of their aggressive driving habits. We process hundreds of these cues from the drivers all around us in milliseconds, without conscious thought. We become mentally prepared for the unexpected, actually knowing it was going to happen beforehand because of this marvelous gift called intuition.

Just as we use intuition while driving, we can use it in leadership. People are constantly giving us cues about their feelings and motivations. If we listen to what they are really saying to us, at the subliminal level, we can solve many problems, before they catch us by surprise.

To further illustrate, have you ever met someone for the first time and had an intuitive feeling about him? You might recognize a potential friend you'd like to know better, or someone to clearly avoid in the future. That's intuition at work. Usually the reasons for these first impressions become evident only later on, as you get to know the person over time. But often, that sixth sense was right on the mark from the very beginning.

As a leader, learn to really listen to that quiet voice within. Trust your intuition. Maybe it's used to make decisions about potential new hires, or to sense a subtle change in one of your employees, or a change in attitude of one of your valued customers. Explore more deeply. Look for underlying answers. Take advantage of what intuition may be telling you. Don't discount your sixth sense just because you don't fully understand the source of its power. It's real; it's working!

BODY LANGUAGE

Psychologists tell us that most of our communication is actually contained in our body language: facial expressions, posture, the eyes, inflection, energy level, etc. Our words themselves carry a very small percentage of the total communication. Wise leaders use their intuition to tune into these nuanced messages by paying close attention to body language.

"Kinesics" is the scientific name for the study of body language.[3] These wordless signals include grooming, hair and clothing styles, and even such practices as tattooing and body piercing. Body language can reveal unspoken information about people's identity, relationships, and thoughts, as well as moods, motivation, and attitudes. It plays an important role in all interpersonal relationships.

Body language can be inborn, learned, or a combination of the two. For example, facial expressions of basic emotions such as anger, fear, disgust, or surprise are found in all cultures and are shared by all human beings. As Mark Twain once said, "Human beings are the only animals who blush—or need to!"[4] Crying, laughing, or shrugging the shoulders have inborn qualities, but they have also been shaped by a particular culture, so they are a combination of the two. Lastly, you have the example of saluting, which is learned behavior only. Contrast the way Julius Caesar's Roman legions saluted, or the British, Nazis, and Americans during World War II and you get the idea.

Recent discoveries in neuroscience have given us other insights into the way human beings process information. Spoken language is a more recent phenomenon in human evolution and has its origins in the cerebral cortex, where higher thinking predominates. On the other hand, body language is spawned in the more primitive areas of the brain, much like our earliest fight-or-flight response to the sudden appearance of a saber-toothed tiger. It is a reflex action that bypasses the thinking brain and is more unguarded and natural. People process nonverbal cues—such as smiling, staring, or clenching of fists—without conscious awareness of doing so.[5]

Body language can also reveal lies or feelings a person is trying to hide. Ancient wise men were right when they said, "The eyes are the window to the soul." Does a person make eye contact or look away? Are his eyes darting about? Does he blush with embarrassment?

If there is ever a lack of congruence between a person's words and his body language, rely on body language. It's much more difficult to conceal.[6]

HISTORY'S LESSONS

History provides many lessons on communication. During the Battle of Trafalgar, Lord Nelson briefed his fleet captains with a simple, broad outline of his battle plan. He purposely avoided spelling it out in minute detail because he wanted his commanders to take advantage of opportunities as they arose during the course of the fight. The Spanish-French fleet, on the other hand, was limited to strict obedience to signal flags from the flagship. However, in the chaos of the ensuing battle, the Spanish and French ships could not even see these flag hoists because they were obscured by dense cannon smoke, onboard fires, and sails, masts, and rigging crashing to the decks. Unable to take independent action without higher direction, they were easily defeated by Nelson's fleet.

At the critical Battle of Gettysburg, General Robert E. Lee lost contact with his cavalry commander, Jeb Stuart. When General Stuart finally appeared, Lee asked him, "Where have you been? Don't you realize you are my eyes and ears?"[7] Without Stuart to communicate the movements of the Union Army, General Lee was at a severe disadvantage. He was a blind man groping in the dark during the most pivotal battle of the Civil War. General Stuart so worshipped Lee that even his commander's subtle, disapproving glance—body language, if you will—thoroughly chastised him. He realized how badly he had let Lee down.[8] Stuart's lack of communication was a factor in the outcome of the battle, and ultimately, the war.

On April 10, 1912, the "unsinkable" HMS *Titanic* set sail on her maiden voyage from Southampton to New York. Either through complacency or hubris, Captain Smith, her commanding officer, failed to heed seven different warnings about icebergs in the North Atlantic. To make matters worse, the bow lookout did not have his binoculars on that fateful night of April 14 and was unable to give adequate warning of the impending collision. At 11:40 p.m., the ill-fated liner struck the iceberg that sealed her fate. She sank in less than three hours with the loss of nearly fifteen hundred men, women, and children.[9]

Just prior to the outbreak of hostilities, Japanese diplomats in Washington D.C. were frantically scrambling to decode the secret message that would declare war on the United States. It was Japan's intent to declare war before the attack on Pearl Harbor, in keeping with the ancient samurai code of Bushido. To attack a sleeping enemy without warning would be a disgrace to that warrior ethic. However, because this critical communication was not delivered in time, the attack became a "day that would live in infamy." Japanese pilots interviewed after the war expressed their feelings of disgrace for violating their own warrior code. In America, reactions to this sneak attack "awakened the sleeping giant" and fueled our resolve for unconditional surrender. That delayed communication changed the course of history.

Historians have noted the marked contrast between the two armies facing each other in Normandy on D-Day, June 6, 1944. On the one hand, the Allies improvised on the fly in response to the chaos they encountered on the beaches. They scrapped their carefully laid out battle plan and quickly adapted to changing conditions without asking permission from higher headquarters. The Germans, on the other hand, could do nothing but follow strict orders. Even though changing conditions warranted different tactics, they were unable to respond without new orders. In the turmoil and fog of war, they lost the initiative to the Allies. In fact, it's been theorized that if the roles were reversed and the Allies were defending the beachhead and the Germans attacking, the invasion would have failed.

On July 30, 1945, shortly after the USS *Indianapolis* had delivered the atomic bomb to the island of Tinian, she was struck by a torpedo fired from the Japanese submarine, *I-58*. The Commanding Officer of the *Indianapolis* was never warned about Japanese submarine activity in the area. As a consequence, he never sailed an evasive course that might have saved his doomed ship. Tragically, the Navy had no procedures in place for filing an itinerary communicating ships' movements. As a result, after she was sunk, Indianapolis was never missed. Only a chance encounter by a Navy patrol plane, which happened to sight survivors during a routine patrol three days after the sinking, led to the rescue of the remaining crew. In all, only 316 men survived out of a crew of 1,199. The rest drowned, died of exposure, or were devoured by sharks.[10]

After the terrorist attacks on the World Trade Center on September 11, 2001, scores of firefighters were lost when those towering skyscrapers collapsed. Sadly, in many cases, it was because they never heard the evacuation order given to them over their radios. Those emergency radios have now been upgraded to more powerful units that can receive transmissions deep within a building. But had better communication been available in 2001, many lives would have been saved.

In September 2003 during manufacture, a $100 million Tiros Satellite was being repositioned from vertical to horizontal on the turnover cart. It slipped off the fixture, causing severe damage. The 18' long spacecraft was about 3' off the ground when it fell. The mishap was caused because twenty-four bolts were missing from a fixture in the turnover cart. Two errors occurred. First, technicians from another satellite program that uses the same type of turnover cart removed the twenty-four bolts without proper documentation. Second, the NOAA team working failed to follow the procedure to verify the configuration of the turnover cart (since they had used it just a few days earlier and assumed nothing had changed). The shock and vibration of the fall caused tremendous damage. Significant rework and retest was required as a result of this very costly miscommunication.[11]

BARRIERS TO COMMUNICATION

There are many barriers to communication. At the most basic level, communication involves a sender, a medium, and a receiver. Breakdowns can occur anywhere along that line. Leaders must always remember that everyone filters the message they both transmit and receive through their own personal worldview and biases. This is just the way humans are wired, and it must be taken into account.

Probably the single greatest enemy of good communication is ego. We are all self-centered to one degree or another. People want to feel important, to be heard, to be top dog, often at the expense of others. This arrogance usually has an intellectual, cultural, racial, gender, age, or power-based origin. Any criterion that sets people apart can be the basis for this bias. A poor leader says to himself, "I'm smarter and more experienced. What could they possibly be able to tell me that I don't already know?" Or perhaps an individual may think, "What could that old man teach me?"

How do we combat this tendency? Often it takes a dose of humility. Once a leader is knocked off his high horse a few times, he learns to listen and take inputs from all sources. If that doesn't wake him up, he won't be leading much longer anyway.

Fear can be another tremendous barrier to good communication. Often it involves saving face, not wanting to look bad, be embarrassed, or humiliated. In fact, in many cultures, saving face is paramount. Sadly, innocent people have been sacrificed for the sake of national pride. The SARS epidemic spread rapidly because the Chinese were unwilling to admit they had a serious problem. The explosion at the Chernobyl nuclear plant was covered up, putting thousands of citizens downwind of the blast at great risk. Many cosmonauts were killed in the Russian space program, but the news was kept classified and the lessons learned a secret.

If leaders and nations could learn to deal openly with their failures, everyone would benefit. Deep down, everyone understands that we are all human and prone to error. Saving face doesn't have to be so important. In fact, people have a greater tolerance for mistakes than we recognize. Genuine honesty and forthrightness would be a breath of fresh air and solve a lot of the world's problems. Humanity could then learn from our collective failures and advance more rapidly.

Other aspects of human nature play major roles in communication. Sometimes there is genuine anger and animosity between the parties involved. It is very hard to communicate with someone we dislike or we feel has wronged us. Even if they have something worthwhile to say, we'll often ignore it and shut off all communication. When dislike turns to hatred, we now have an explosive situation, and dialogue is impossible.

Until we can begin to talk in terms of our common humanity, what we both value, there is little chance of agreement. Seeking that common ground, however difficult, is the only way real progress can be made. The situation in the Middle East is a tragic example of this. Both sides are blinded by hatred and revenge. Unless and until they can sit down and focus on the parallel teachings of their two great religions, and what they share in common, peace and harmony will never be achieved.

Sometimes poor communication is the fault of the medium. It can't handle the distance or the volume. Think of the evolution of a letter carried from New York to San Francisco by clipper ship, then by pony express, later telegraph, airplane, fax, and now e-mail. Sometimes that increasing capability actually becomes a liability and we have circuit overload. Look at the deluge of e-mails in your in-box every morning. The ease of sending them has overwhelmed the ability to respond to them.

The solution lies in being more discriminating in our communication. We need to pause and decide what's really important before we speak—or hit the send button. We can all see ourselves in the mirror when it comes to this problem. We should also rediscover the importance of silence. In fact, a silent pause can make the difference between an inspiring speech and noisy demagoguery. At times, saying nothing at all is the best course of action.

In the end, good communication is achieved by following the Golden Rule, being considerate of those receiving our message. By combining compassion and awareness, we will be able to notice when someone is not in a receptive mood. Perhaps they have just experienced the death of a loved one or some other event in their lives that makes it impossible to listen. A kind, "I'm sorry, I see I've caught you at a bad time" works wonders. If we set that example in our own communication, there's a good chance that others will reciprocate.

REFLECTION AND DISCUSSION

1. Do you consider communication to be an essential leadership skill? Can you lead without it?

2. Are good listening skills lacking in most leaders today? Is there value in being the last to speak?

3. What roles do intuition and body language play in communication?

4. Give some examples of barriers to communication, either from history or your own personal experiences.

Chapter 8
Empowerment

"COME FOLLOW ME, AND I WILL MAKE YOU FISHERS OF MEN."

MARK 1:17

True empowerment begins with one very powerful idea: There is no one like you in the entire universe. You are a unique creation, and the one who created you always does fantastic work. Every human being is a masterpiece. It is impossible for Him to do anything less.

The trouble starts when we forget this fundamental truth about all human beings and ourselves. Instead, we become highly critical, denying the extraordinary creations we are. We begin to compare ourselves to others, either becoming jealous that we don't measure up, or arrogant, thinking we're better than everyone else. It's a total waste of time and energy because it overlooks each person's uniqueness. In other words, there really is no basis for comparison. You're not better, you're not worse, you are simply *you*. No one like you has ever existed, and no one ever will.

BARRIERS TO EMPOWERMENT

Ego is often a barrier to empowerment—and frequently *the* barrier. It sabotages empowerment in several ways. It is usually the reason we are highly critical of others. From our lofty position, they fall short of our arbitrary standards. Ego can also activate our defense mechanisms. We feel insecure and therefore compelled to belittle others to make up for our own perceived shortcomings. It's the only way we can stay on top.

Ego may also be the reason insecure leaders hoard power. They cannot deal with others as equals and feel that sharing power will lessen their hold on it. They fail to see that power shared is actually power multiplied.

Fear is another major barrier to empowerment—often entangled with ego as well. We might be afraid of making a mistake or looking foolish, so we don't even try, dismissing the attempt as too difficult or too risky to one's self-esteem. Or, our fear of failure may prompt us to exercise total control over a project rather than risk the consequences of a subordinate's error. People working for us become gun shy and frustrated because of our micro-managing leadership style. This stifles creativity throughout the team.

Negative thinking destroys empowerment, for others and us. The game is lost before it even begins. Whatever you think, you're right! Your negative thoughts about failure or losing become the proverbial self-fulfilling prophecies. Your thoughts of disaster and impending doom create a blueprint, which your subconscious, goal-directed mind, unerringly achieves in reality. Sadly, you're using your natural, inborn creativity to pursue negative goals.

HARNESSING THE POWER WITHIN

Start harnessing the power within by promising yourself to avoid needless criticism and negative thoughts, directed at yourself or others. They serve no purpose and sabotage morale. Instead, substitute positive thoughts for negative ones. In other words, reprogram your mental computer. Granted, it's not an easy task. But remember, it took years to fill your mind with negativity, so it will take just as long to do a thorough housecleaning.

Be optimistic and look on the bright side. Even when the world seems to be crashing down around you, assume the attitude, "It really isn't that bad." It's all in your perspective. Consider this: A disaster for an American is a power outage that forces him to eat the food in his refrigerator before it spoils. A disaster for a Chinese peasant is having a monsoon annihilate his entire village, killing ten thousand other countrymen, and having to face starvation.

Use your mistakes as learning tools. The human mind is designed to process error for one purpose only: future benefit and personal growth. Mistakes should never become objectives in themselves. Don't dwell on mistakes or you'll become a perpetual victim, and that makes you believe you are powerless. Just remember, you're human. Expect failure. Learn from it and move on.

Let's be honest, we're all afraid at one time or another. But don't let fear paralyze you. Most of our fears never materialize anyway. And if they do, not to the degree we anticipated. Besides, you're never alone. You always have a support network of family, friends, and a loving God. Don't be embarrassed or afraid to reach for a life ring when you need it. One day you'll return the favor and provide one for someone else.

THE POWER OF BELIEVING

Believe in yourself! Start with the premise that you are already creative by nature. You have a wonderful instrument, the human mind, standing by to do your bidding. It merely waits to be programmed with your visions. Believe the answer already exists. Think of the solution as a phone number that you've only temporarily forgotten. Perhaps this sounds like magic or voodoo. But it can be described only as amazing, and it works! Let me illustrate.

Henry Ford was convinced that his engineers could build a V-8 engine. At the time, it didn't even exist. His engineers said it was "impossible." So what did Ford do? He simply locked them in a room and told them to design one. In his own mind he already knew it could be done. A few days later, his engineers emerged with a V-8, just as Ford had envisioned. He believed in them, and that was enough to empower them to create it.

In May of 1961, John F. Kennedy startled the nation, and certainly NASA engineers, with a speech proclaiming that the goal of this nation should be to put a man on the moon, and return him safely to Earth, before the end of the decade. No doubt, the jaws of many NASA engineers hit the floor! "Why, we haven't even put a man in space, let alone sent him to the moon!" they said. But Kennedy's vision rallied the nation and everyone involved with the space program. He challenged them with a goal, created the possibility long before it became a reality, and that's all it took. He made them believers.

The four-minute mile had always been an impossible barrier until Roger Bannister broke it in 1954. Suddenly, once that psychological barrier had been shattered, many more runners were able to run a mile in under four minutes. In reality, the only thing holding back those other runners had been their lack of belief that it could be done.

The human mind is a phenomenal instrument. It will achieve any goal when programmed properly with your creative imagination. If, for example, your goal is to improve foul shooting, it will learn from every shot you miss and every shot you make. What is most interesting, however, is that while you may initially miss many more than you make, the mind pays more attention to its successes than its failures. In other words, it focuses on success and uses failure only as a stepping-stone to achieve a higher success rate. That is why it is foolish to lament our failures. The mind is programmed only to learn from them, then forget them as it homes in on its primary goal: success.

When you experience a low point in your life and are feeling discouraged and perhaps overwhelmed, stop and remember your past successes. In fact, that's exactly what Jimmy Stewart did in the classic movie, *It's a Wonderful Life*. By seeing the positive impact he had had on other people's lives, his spirit was renewed. His entire outlook changed and his optimism returned when he focused on success.

We have been programmed for success, not failure. Believe it!

JUST SHOOT THE BALL

Empowerment comes when we decide to commit ourselves wholeheartedly and let go of any doubts about the outcome.

Athletes describe this as being "in the zone." As soon as you become overly concerned with the outcome, looking nervously up at the scoreboard, you become shackled by doubt. Performance suffers and you depart the zone. This happens every time you overthink. Thinking is fine when first analyzing a problem. But once the decision is made on a course of action, get your thinking mind out of the way and let your creative mind take over.

Robert Horry of the Los Angeles Lakers had an uncanny ability to make game-winning shots at the final buzzer. After another one of his last second baskets gave his team the victory, he was asked by reporters, "What do you think about when you get the ball in those critical situations?" Robert replied, "I can't think; if I did, I'd miss. I just have to react and let my body take over."

We've all heard of "paralysis through analysis." It's just what Robert was talking about. Do you think Pete Sampras thinks about how high to toss the tennis ball when he serves? Of course not! He just throws it up and hits it.

Granted, it takes years of training to create that kind of automatic response, or muscle memory. But often, after we've reached that level of training, we start second-guessing ourselves. Our minds allow self-doubt to creep in instead of just allowing all that training to "flow" naturally, unencumbered by thinking.

Did you ever notice how basketball teams sometimes shoot very poorly in the opening minutes of a championship game? The reason: They're thinking too much and worrying about making mistakes instead of just going out and enjoying the competitive challenge.

How about you? Are you able to let go and let your training take over? Or are you allowing your mind's negative self-talk to take you out of the zone? When you make a mistake, are you able to leave it in the past where it belongs, or do you let it hinder your performance in the present?

SWING FOR THE FENCES

One of the most decorated fighting units of World War II was the 100th Battalion of the 442 Infantry Regiment, composed entirely of Nisei soldiers, second generation Japanese-Americans.[1]

These were amazing fighting men. Even though many of their family members were being held in Japanese internment camps back in the United States, they fought valiantly for their country against the Germans in Europe. Their bravery was so renowned that they were also known as "The Purple Heart Battalion."

"Go for broke" was the 442's motto because these legendary soldiers gave every last measure of themselves in battle. They were tenacious and unstoppable.

Babe Ruth was one of the greatest home run hitters in baseball history. To see him swing at a pitch gave true meaning to the words, "Swing for the fences." Babe held nothing back. While hitting all those home runs, he also led the league in strikeouts, but that never discouraged him. He wasn't afraid of failure. He was never tentative at the plate. He knew that failure goes hand in hand with great achievement, just as the 442 knew that victory often meant the ultimate sacrifice.

Are you willing to swing for the fences? Can you commit to your vision and put it all on the line, holding nothing back? Remember, half-hearted efforts usually end in failure.

MENTORING

Throughout history, inspiring mentors have empowered others. They passed on their knowledge to the next generation. Adam, no doubt, taught Cain and Abel how to hunt and till the soil.

The entire guild system of the Middle Ages worked that way. A man, under the guidance of a great master, progressed from apprentice, to journeyman, and finally to master himself.

The military works the same way. In fact, one of the Command-ing Officer's greatest responsibilities is mentoring his sailors and officers. If he does the job properly, many will become Chief Petty Officers and Commanding Officers themselves one day.

In the martial arts, a Sensei provides instruction to his students as they progress from one colored belt to the next. Flight instruc-tors have a similar relationship with their students. It is a tried and true system.

But great mentors and coaches do more than just instruct in physical skills. They teach life lessons. John Wooden was a great basketball coach. But he is far more revered by his former players as one of the greatest life mentors they've ever known. Vince Lombardi was a legend to his players for the same reason. Both coaches taught life skills, indelibly etched in their athletes' minds forever.

Perhaps no other mentoring role is more important than that of a parent because so much is at stake. Children are sent down their initial path in life by the values they learn from mom and dad. In those early years, they are the most impressionable. They soak up everything. Jesus himself warns those who would give a bad example to a child, "It would be better for him that a mill-stone were hanged about his neck, and that he were drowned in the depth of the sea."[2] The prosperity—or demise—of a nation of-ten depends on the quality of family life and the mentoring that children receive.

SECRETS OF EMPOWERING LEADERS

Empowering leaders must be role models. They have to set an example that inspires people to follow them. Saint Francis of Assisi said to his missionaries before sending them abroad to preach the gospel, "Go forth and teach them, and if you must, use words." That succinctly captures the whole point: Example is the most important tool a leader has. People care little about what you say; but they will follow you to the ends of the Earth based on what you do and who you are.

Inspiring leaders are patient teachers and mentors. They generously provide one of their most important gifts: time. A young, inexperienced intern working in a large hospital, exhausted after long hours on call, needs to know that the chief resident is readily available, standing by to provide support and answer any questions he may have about patient care. A good football coach runs a play over and over again in practice, until his players know their blocking assignments and pass routes. When they make mistakes, he patiently corrects them. The best coaches seldom have to raise their voices. Their body language and facial expressions tell all. Coaches who have to yell all the time become "screamers" that players soon tune out. Parents can fall into this same trap if nagging is all they do. Children respond much better to calm, patient mentoring.

Wise leaders know that learning new skills is empowering. They are constantly working on self-improvement and urging their followers to expand their horizons as well. They promote outside education even when it doesn't directly relate to the job, often at company expense, to broaden employees' knowledge and enrich their lives. They know it sends a powerful message that they care about their people, and a more educated team is a better team. Enlightened leaders may also provide recommended reading lists, because they know that great books contain great wisdom.

Inspiring leaders share power. It takes real courage to stand aside and play a supporting role, giving others a chance to lead. But that's the only way subordinates will ever learn to be leaders themselves. Sometimes the boss must bite his tongue and even allow mistakes to happen, fighting the urge to take over. For example, it would be very easy for the Commanding Officer of a Navy squadron to lead all the flights and take the best missions. But if his junior pilots are ever going to learn how to lead, the CO must step aside. Often it means the CO serves as a wingman for his junior officers on a flight mission. This builds their confidence.

If mistakes are made, or even a fiasco should occur, a leader must then become a mentor, patiently pointing out the lessons learned, but avoiding sharp criticism. Sometimes a leader's greatest resource is his own memory of how he blew it himself when he first tried. By humbly sharing his own failed attempt, he can teach a great lesson, offer encouragement, and restore confidence at the same time.

Leadership consultant Michele Jackman tells us that when the boss relinquishes the reins of power to encourage junior leaders, it is essential that they be provided these things: "authority to act without second guessing, access to essential information, the resources and tools needed, the training and coaching necessary to meet the leader's expectations, and the guaranteed accountability of others." If any of these is missing, the boss has severely handicapped the future leader he is trying to develop. It is a prescription for failure and may discourage any future subordinates from attempting to take on a leadership role.

Encouragement and positive feedback empower people in an extraordinary way. When that affirmation comes from someone highly respected, it is even more powerful. A young Mickey Mantle was awed by the help he received from one of the greatest centerfielders of all time, Joe Dimaggio. Barry Bonds was mentored by two Hall of Famers, his dad, Bobby, and Willie Mays (who also happened to be his godfather). Wayne Gretzky received the torch from Gordy Howe. Tiger Woods voluntarily mentors young kids. Can you imagine what it means to a seven-year-old to be taught how to grip a golf club by the best golfer in the world!

My daughter, Molly, when she was four years old, used to ask, "Dad, will you color with me?" She'd sit on the floor next to me, using my footstool as a desk, and we would color together for hours. Often we would draw animals, her favorite subjects. After a couple of years of coloring together, my horse still looked like a pregnant hippopotamus, but Molly's was anatomically perfect, even showing all the muscles and sinews in correct proportion. It could have passed for Secretariat. I laughed and told her, "Molly, you've passed me by as an artist"—a little embarrassing since she was only six years old at the time.

She remembers those words to this day. I suppose they might have had more impact had I been any kind of an artist at all, but they still encouraged her. Molly went on to win a scholarship in fine arts and biology at the University of California at Irvine.

We can all remember our children's first tentative steps. We waited anxiously as they stood up, then awkwardly tottered toward us. Our outstretched arms and words of encouragement—"You can do it!"—cheered them on.

That same positive environment is equally important in our adult world. Just as we showed confidence in our children's hesitant attempts to walk, we need to affirm those who are looking to us for leadership, encouragement, and inspiration. Recognize the talent and brilliance around you, even if it eclipses your own. Never miss a chance to acknowledge good effort. And even more important, be ready to console those who fail. Then teach them how to succeed. Helping others reach their dreams is one of the greatest rewards a leader can have.

BE "OTHERS-CENTERED"

Viktor Frankl said it best: To be in total harmony with our guiding principles and to reach our full potential as human beings we need to be "transcendent."[3] This means being centered on others, putting them above our own selfish interests.

A surprising thing happens when we do this: We actually increase our own joy. We make life fun, for others and ourselves. We begin to recognize the hidden talents of those around us and to acknowledge that they may actually have a better way of doing things. We become more tolerant and forgiving. We learn that basic goodness can shine for others as a guiding beacon. Ultimately, we discover that our *love* provides them with the highest form of empowerment. It is then that we can truly leave a legacy for others.

REFLECTION AND DISCUSSION

1. Name three barriers to empowerment and tell why you selected them.

2. Mistakes can be great empowerment tools. Do you agree or disagree?

3. What role does creative imagination play in empowerment?

4. How does fear affect empowerment?

5. Name your four most empowering role models and tell why you selected them.

Chapter 9
Decisiveness

"MAN IS BY NO MEANS MERELY A PRODUCT OF HEREDITY AND
ENVIRONMENT. THERE IS ANOTHER ELEMENT: DECISION. MAN
ULTIMATELY DECIDES FOR HIMSELF! AND, IN THE END, EDUCATION
MUST BE EDUCATION TOWARD THE ABILITY TO DECIDE."

VIKTOR FRANKL

Decisiveness is fundamental to good leadership. While avoiding a tough choice may seem like a temporary escape from responsibility, doing nothing is itself a decision and will have consequences.

At the same time, leaders need to be wary of subordinates who present them with only two options, neither one palatable, but expecting the leader to decide right now. This should set off alarm bells. At this point, a leader's intuition should tell him to ask about other options not yet considered. Often the unexplored alternative ends up being the right way to go.

Never think that being the boss makes you right. If this is your attitude, get ready for a large helping of humble pie. Many times

I've been the pilot of a Navy helicopter on a low-level navigation flight. Three of us on board agreed we were in one position, but the fourth crewman had calculated our position somewhere else. We listened to his reasoning (which was based on what he saw from looking at the surrounding terrain). He pointed out terrain features we had missed. Sure enough, that one crewman was right, but we never would have gotten back on track if we had ignored him.

Making decisions is not often easy. But there is no requirement to fly solo. Surround yourself with good people and let them contribute. Create a "brain trust" of advisors. Gather as much information as you can from numerous perspectives and pay particular attention to devil's advocates. First, they are demonstrating courage, a quality you want on your team. Second, their contrary opinion may be just the answer you're looking for.

Stephen Covey reminds us to make a habit of looking for a win-win and the common good in our decisions.[1] Be flexible, get out of the rut, and let go of old ideas if they are holding you back. Make the best decision you can based on the available facts. Don't rush it, but if you're waiting for a complete picture to emerge before deciding, you'll never make *any* decisions. As the Nike ad says, "Just do it." Further waiting may result only in a missed opportunity.

Eventually, you'll reach a point where deliberation and planning have to end, and it's time to make a decision. As Eisenhower realized before launching the D-Day invasion at Normandy, very few decisions are ever absolute certainties. Those aren't decisions anyway. They're forgone conclusions, easy to make. Where would be the leadership challenge in that? A tough decision, however, takes courage.

Perhaps we're paralyzed by the fear of failure or the neurotic pursuit of perfection. But we're human. We're going to make mistakes. In fact, no great achievement was ever realized without many mistakes being made along the way. Mistakes are the keys to progress of any kind.

Once you make a decision, let go and commit to it. Swing for the fences. That will help you relax, put you in the zone, and give you the greatest chance of success. Regret and second-guessing are a total waste of energy. If you end up being wrong, so what? Admit it, and then make the correction. Remember: "Take note of where you stumble; that's where the treasure lies." Only growth and learning count. Having that attitude will diminish the fear of making decisions.

VIKTOR FRANKL ON DECISION-MAKING

Mankind's search for happiness is actually a search for peace, that "pearl of great price." Ultimately, peace means freedom from our lower instincts, heredity, and environment.

We once thought that our fate was preordained, that we had little control over our lives or what we were destined to become. But more recently we have discovered that man can exercise a remarkable degree of control. While our instincts and heredity certainly influence us, we have an amazing ability to override them through our own decisions.

In a similar way, we control our environment; it does not control us. Viktor Frankl was living proof of this. Forced to suffer the most horrific conditions imaginable in a Nazi concentration camp, he was still able to exercise personal freedom in response to his environment. In fact, he chose to behave in a way that actually gave him more freedom than the sadistic Nazi guards who imprisoned him. Dr. Frankl chose to maintain a positive, humanitarian attitude, whereas they lost their free will, enslaved by their own savagery and ruthlessness.

"Few of us," Frankl says, "make important life choices with any degree of decisiveness. Backtracking here and compromising there, we often lack the backbone to stand by our own decisions. Because of this, we remain in a continual state of angst. At times we hold a wandering, day-to-day attitude toward whatever comes our way. At others we are fatalistic, defeatist. One day we exhibit spinelessness and have no clearly defined opinion at all; the next we cling so strongly and stubbornly to an idea we become fanatical. Ultimately," Frankl continues, "all these symptoms can be traced back to our fear of responsibility, and the indecision which is its fruit."[2]

GENERAL WALTER BOOMER

There is a common belief that on the battlefield there is no time for collaboration. It is thought that quick decisions must be made by one, solitary commander, a tactical genius, prescient and all-seeing, able to make instantaneous judgments. That is a myth.

General Boomer, the Marine Corps Ground Commander during Desert Storm, would tell you that a successful commander does it differently. He creates an inner circle of experienced battlefield advisors and listens very carefully to their inputs. He would be an absolute fool to devise a complex plan on his own. Of course, the final decision is always his to make, but it is never done in a vacuum. The more complex the battle plan, the greater the collaboration and deliberation needed before a final decision is made.

Leaders who ignore this advice and try to go it alone end up like George Armstrong Custer at the Battle of the Little Bighorn, victims of their own hubris, needlessly sacrificing men's lives.

CONSCIENCE

Every one of us has a little voice deep inside that never lies to us. It lets us know if what we're doing is morally right. We can choose not to listen, but it is still undeniably there. It critiques our every move. It is a powerful aid to great leaders when they listen to it. It gives moral resonance to their decisions. We frequently wrestle with it, rationalize with it, or outright ignore and stifle it. But conscience is very resilient and keeps telling us the truth, whether we listen or not.

So why are we talking about it here? Simply because disaster often happens when we stray from the advice of this most subtle voice within. And also, over time, if we ignore our conscience too often, its voice becomes too weak to be heard anymore. At that point, a leader has lost his most important ally. Without a moral compass, good leadership and decision-making are impossible.

John Winter wrote that the most fruitful chapters of his life were those he entered with a firm decision—and the intention of sticking to it, come what may:

"It was the first time I really had to choose between my own wishes and what my conscience was telling me to do. I can say only now, fifty-eight years later, that at that moment I experienced something of the peace given by God. I have had to think of it several times since then in my life, when my conscience has prodded me to take a step I didn't want to take at first. Each time I followed my conscience, it has led to an inner peace, which is absolutely true and cannot be described. On the other side of the coin, life has also made me realize that if you hear a call but don't follow, it does something to you inside, and maybe the next time God speaks, you will not be able to hear him as clearly."[3]

Some choices are easy to make. Some require agonizing soul-searching. Here is where God can help us. Leave the solution in His hands. It may not come quickly like a thunderclap, but more often like a whisper over a long period of time. But you will recognize the answer by the feeling of peace that accompanies it.

Henri J. M. Nouwen may have said it best: "Deciding to do this, that, or the other for the next five, ten, or twenty years is no great decision. Turning fully, unconditionally, and without fear to God is. Yet this awareness sets me free."[4]

GO WITH YOUR GUT

We talked about intuition before and what a marvelous gift it is. Some may call it that "inner voice," "instinct," or "sixth sense." Perhaps it's actually our conscience at work. Whatever we may call it, it is our strongest ally in the decision-making process. When good information—or "intelligence" on the battlefield—is unavailable, go with your gut. Years of experience have honed it into a sharp tool. Use it!

When inspiring leaders are asked, "How were you able to make such a difficult decision?" they often answer, "I just did what I thought was right." Surely the leaders at Enron could not have felt good about what they were doing. Yet they ignored their consciences and led thousands of employees into bankruptcy. They forgot the simple advice Walt Disney's cartoon character, Jimminy Cricket, once told us as children, "Always let your conscience be your guide."

Doctor James Gonzales, from the Class of 1971, gives this dramatic account of a defining moment where he truly followed his conscience in order to make a tough decision:

"I was a brand new surgical intern. Around midnight one evening, a thirty-something male was transported to the E.R. with a shotgun wound to the face. The patient's entire face, including both eyes, was missing. Frantically we stabilized him in the E.R. before transporting him to the O.R. Several hours into the surgery, word came that the patient was a suicide attempt. Furthermore, the patient had recently been diagnosed with a terminal brain tumor. When several members of the O.R. team hinted that maybe it would be better if the patient died on the operating table, the chief surgical resident looked at me and asked, 'Dr. Gonzales, he's your patient, what do you think?' My reply was that even though the patient had made a suicide attempt, we had a moral, ethical, and legal duty to save the patient's life. The patient survived his surgery. About nine months later he died from his inoperable brain tumor."

Dr. Gonzales made the right decision. We can never know the good that can be accomplished by a single human being in whatever time he has remaining on this Earth. Good works and demonstrated courage can inspire untold numbers of people who might never have been influenced. Or perhaps it gives an individual a chance to make peace with his Creator before he dies. Life is a choice that God makes, not man.

Alan Ptak, currently President/CEO of Syntegra Federal, from the Class of 1971, describes two examples that served as his personal benchmarks for ethical decision-making. The first concerns his mentor, Norm Augustine, who was then President and CEO of Martin Marietta.

Martin Marietta built a spacecraft called the Mars Observer. Its task was to orbit Mars and send valuable data back to Earth. The contract included significant incentive awards for reaching specific milestones, which could add up to a total of $25 million. The first milestone was a successful launch on time in 1993. The second milestone was to reach Earth orbit, and the last, to reach Mars orbit. The Mars Observer met all its objectives, including Mars orbit.

But soon after that, it was never heard from again. According to the contract, the milestones were made, even though the orbiter then went out of control. In spite of that failure, NASA made the incentive payments to Martin Marietta without contesting them.

So what did Norm Augustine and his company do? They gave the money back! They had every legal right to keep every penny, but the CEO felt the decision did not pass "the smell test."

There is an interesting epilogue to this story: Morale at Martin Marietta soared to new heights because of their leader's decision. It set a sterling example for ethical conduct and became part of the company's culture.

Alan Ptak's second story involves the Central Intelligence Agency and the Navy's attempt to clandestinely recover a Soviet golf class submarine using the *Glomar Explorer*. Prior to the actual raising of the stricken sub, the focus was on the military value of highly classified material onboard and insight into Soviet capabilities. No advanced consideration was made concerning human remains, which might be discovered.

During the actual covert recovery northeast of Hawaii in the Central Pacific, human remains were discovered. This posed an ethical dilemma. Should the recovery team secretly dump the bodies to cover up this intelligence gold mine? Certainly, no one would be the wiser—the Soviets or the American public.

Instead, the Director of the CIA and the Chief of Naval Operations decided to conduct a proper burial at sea with full military honors. The entire ceremony was videotaped. They took the extra time to do the right thing with a burial at sea, in spite of the increased risk of detection and discovery.

BE READY TO STAND ALONE

After considering all inputs, decisiveness often boils down to courage, the common good, and your guiding principles. The toughest decisions may even require you to stand alone, abandoned by everyone else. But you must do what is right, regardless of the consequences. You may be ridiculed, scorned, or ostracized—but so what! That's often the price you pay for following your conscience.

General Robert E. Lee was faced with a dilemma. The Confederate cause was lost, but many thousands of his men were still ready to follow him in a long, protracted guerilla campaign. Lee realized that if he led such a campaign, it would be bloody and countless additional soldiers would die. Worse yet, the gaping national wound of the Civil War would not heal for many more years to come. Surrender was not in his vocabulary. But for the good of the country, to see North and South reunited once more, he convinced his army to lay down their arms, return to their farms and families, and begin the long rebuilding process. Only a man of Lee's stature and influence, revered by his soldiers and throughout the South, could make that happen, and he knew it. They would not quit unless he gave the order, so he set aside his personal feelings and chose what was best for the country.

Branch Rickey knew that integrating major league baseball would cause a firestorm of protest.[5] He was fully aware of the anger and outrage that would result from his decision, bringing out the ugliest side of human nature. Furthermore, he knew that this momentous decision needed a courageous partner. Branch Rickey found that in the character of Jackie Robinson. He told Jackie what he would have to endure. Jackie simply replied, "I have two cheeks, Mr. Rickey." The courage of these two men changed major league baseball—and our nation—forever.

Jewish psychiatrist Viktor Frankl could see the Nazi noose tightening around his beloved Austria. He had a difficult choice to make: leave the country while there was still time, or stay and look after his aging parents, who were too old to flee. He chose to stay, even though he knew it was a probable death sentence for him. Because of his unconquerable spirit—and a few random twists of fate—Dr. Frankl survived the Nazi death camps and lived to tell about it in his monumental book, *Man's Search for Meaning*. By following the teachings learned long ago in his youth, "Honor thy father and thy mother," he made a courageous choice few others would have made.[6]

President Harry Truman knew in his heart that it was time to integrate the armed forces. In spite of the demonstrated bravery of segregated units in several wars, especially the recent victory in

World War II, minorities such as the Japanese and African Americans were still isolated from the mainstream military establishment. In 1948, Truman issued Executive Order 9981, which called for equality of treatment and opportunity for all members of the military.[7] In 1949, the U.S. Air Force became the first armed service to integrate its units. Even though Truman met with resistance from several senior military leaders, he knew it was the right thing to do and took action in spite of their protests.

Rosa Parks, Martin Luther King, and James Meredith showed similar resolve. They stood tall during those turbulent times when America failed to live up to her promise of "life, liberty, and the pursuit of happiness" for all citizens. They, along with many other African Americans, literally put their lives on the line in the face of mindless hatred. We are a better country today because of their courage.

In October 1973, at the height of the Watergate scandal, President Nixon ordered Attorney General Elliot L. Richardson to fire Special Prosecutor Archibald Cox. Nixon knew that Cox was getting too close to uncovering the President's complicity in the scandal and subsequent cover-up. He also feared that his "dirty tricks" and numerous other violations of the Constitution would be exposed. On principle, Richardson refused to carry out the President's order and tendered his resignation instead. Nixon then ordered the Deputy Attorney General, William D. Ruckelshaus, to fire Cox. He also resigned rather than comply with the President's unlawful order.[8] Their courageous actions followed what generations of midshipmen have been taught at the Naval Academy, reflected in the words of Commodore Matthew Fontaine Maury in 1849, "When principle is involved, be deaf to expediency."[9]

In the end, history will vindicate courageous leaders who make selfless decisions according to their principles.

DECISIVENESS, ANOTHER PERSPECTIVE

We've made a strong case for decisiveness. But let's explore another perspective that may seem contradictory: Sometimes indecisiveness has great merit.

How can this be? Simply, new learning requires a departure from strongly held beliefs. For example, Charles Darwin startled the world with his ideas about evolution. But his discovery became the unifying theory for biology. It explained things that once baffled scientists and made sense of the living world.

On the other hand, if we convince ourselves there is a sound barrier, which aircraft can never exceed, or that man can't break the four-minute mile, we've set our own limitations. We've shut ourselves off to possibilities, the better mousetrap. We stifle our own human nature that thrives on exploration and discovery.

Man is by nature curious. When allowed to question hidebound beliefs, he becomes open to new and amazing possibilities. "The fact is, we never need to make decisions," John Lienhard at the University of Houston tells us. "What we need to do is to take action. But that's not the same thing at all. A house is burning, and a child is trapped. We inform ourselves as best we can. Then we choose either to break in a window or to enter by the door. We don't decide; we act, because time grants no further choices. We leave decisions to Monday-morning quarterbacks.

"There's always a better way, a better solution. We act, we make choices. But leave decisions to people who need the psychological comfort they provide. The only real closure we'll ever get is death. The glorious indecision is life itself—the sure knowledge that if we can live with ambiguity, we'll live better, have a lot more fun, and ultimately will make that better mousetrap."[10]

REFLECTION AND DISCUSSION

1. What factors make decision-making difficult?

2. Viktor Frankl says that our ability to choose sets us apart as human beings. Do you agree, or do you think we are simply products of heredity and environment?

3. Do you feel that combat still allows room for collaboration or do you think one leader should "take charge"?

4. What role should conscience and guiding principles play in making decisions?

5. What are your thoughts on "glorious indecision"? Is living with ambiguity of value?

Chapter 10
Fairness and Consistency

"BUT THERE'S A DEEPER PROBLEM: PERFECT ENFORCEMENT OF
RULES IS BY ITS NATURE UNFAIR...FAIRNESS MEANS KNOWING
WHEN TO MAKE EXCEPTIONS. AFTER ALL, APPLYING RULES
EQUALLY IS EASY. ANY BUREAUCRAT CAN DO IT. IT'S FAR HARDER
TO KNOW WHEN TO BEND OR EVEN IGNORE THE RULES."

DAVID WEINBERGER

Without fairness and consistency, good leadership is impossible. Teams and organizations must know, without ambiguity or doubt, what their leader stands for—and won't stand for. They must be able to count on the boss. Steady leadership creates high morale and leads to outstanding team performance.

Most revealing is what the team does when the boss is away. A great team will be true to their guiding principles and philosophy, without hesitation, even in the leader's absence. It is the surest way of knowing that these principles have penetrated to the very marrow of the organization.

A leader who is always fair and consistent establishes a culture where followers always know what to expect—and what's expected. The team will then take the initiative and make their own decisions based on the established philosophy, often without the boss even knowing that they've done so. In the Navy, for example, you'll hear them say such things as, "The Skipper wouldn't go for that," or "That's what we stand for here," then taking the appropriate action. This gives the team continuity without the leader even being present.

On the other hand, weak and vacillating policy undermines morale. The team is rudderless. They don't know from one day to the next what will happen or what to expect from their leader. They become hesitant and unsure of themselves. The organization drifts aimlessly.

Even worse is the leader whose behavior is ruled by mood swings. We've all worked for bosses we steered clear of at certain times, depending on their mood. Sometimes we would ask the Skipper's secretary, "Is now a good time to meet with the CO?" Her answer, and the look on her face, shouted, "No!" So we would leave and wait for a better time, perhaps after he had had his morning coffee.

In the worst cases, there would never be a good time to approach him. This environment is uncomfortable to work in, saps morale, and keeps the team off balance. The boss's mood invariably filters down through the rest of the organization and creates uneasiness and uncertainty. While these examples may be drawn from the Navy, they parallel the experiences of people in any organization.

CONSISTENCY, A CRITICAL LEADERSHIP TRAIT

Why is consistency critical to great leadership? Simply because it implies an absence of contradictions. People always know what to expect from a leader who is consistent. On the other hand, a leader who changes with the weather creates insecurity and uneasiness. When you eradicate contradictions in your moral standards, actions, and values, you will eliminate inconsistency.

For example, a father may preach the evils of racial prejudice to his children. But then one day, his teenage daughter is asked to the prom by a Filipino classmate. He tells her not to go with the boy. At that very moment he has given a mixed message. This contradiction undermines everything he has ever told his daughter about racial equality. It has revealed his true feelings and uncovered his hypocrisy.

As we discussed in Chapter Two, when your leadership is consistent and has no contradictions, you have "integrity." An old expression for integrity is "solid gold." You are pure gold through and through with no imperfections, no base metals to taint your character. People with integrity are always true to their beliefs. As Polonius said to his son, Laertes, in Shakespeare's *Hamlet*, "This above all else, to thine own self be true, and it must follow, as the night the day, thou canst not then be false to any man."[1]

Most often our inconsistencies are exposed when our actions contradict what we say. We might claim to be law abiding, but then cheat on our income taxes. Perhaps we feel that cash payments or tips don't have to be reported as income, only because we can get away with it. After all, who would know? But integrity, much like ethics, is "what you do when no one is watching." I think we've all failed that test in our lives at one time or another. But by being mindful of our internal contradictions—our failures of integrity— we can begin the improvement process. Much like the smelting of gold, it takes exposure to the white-hot forge of honest self-appraisal to remove these impurities in our own character.

FAIRNESS RECOGNIZES THE WORTH OF EACH INDIVIDUAL

We undermine fairness and consistency when we blindly apply the rules without considering individuals or circumstances. Initiatives such as mandatory sentencing have exacerbated this problem. Once you remove the discretion of the judge, you have a cookbook legal system. The judge is forced to look up the crime, and then apply the mandatory sentence. He is not allowed to take anything else into account when administering punishment. This is wrong.

No two people are the same, no two sets of circumstances are the same, and no two offenses are the same. If they were, you wouldn't need judges, only bureaucrats. Ideally, we make men and women judges because of their wisdom. If we take away their discretion in applying the law, we've taken away their most important tool and made them powerless.

This idea applies to leaders, coaches, and parents as well. For example, a good coach knows that some players need a good swift kick in the butt to get their attention, but others would be devastated and lose confidence with such methods. Everyone must be motivated in a unique way, and the best leaders know which one to use. Wise parents are also aware that each of their children must be nurtured in a different way. That doesn't mean the parents play favorites—the rules of the family apply equally to all—just that the approach to each child is different. Employing a "one size fits all" method is a failure of leadership.

People want to be treated as unique individuals and to know that their leader cares for each of them in a personal way. No one wants to be lumped into a single, faceless category where individuality is lost. While it may seem to be a contradiction—we first think that everyone should be treated exactly the same way—fairness is best served when these unique, one-on-one relationships are valued and preserved.

WHAT ALL GREAT COACHES KNOW

Phil Jackson, one of the NBA's greatest coaches, learned a valuable lesson early in his coaching career. As he tells it, he made the mistake of letting his star player receive special treatment. It literally tore the team apart. Catering to this prima donna destroyed team morale and ruined team cohesion. A climate of fairness was lost, and jealousy and animosity soon ruled the locker room. Needless to say, the team had an abysmal season. Phil swore he would never make that mistake again, and as a result, he has set a record for coaching excellence.[2] Much of that success is based on his fair and consistent policies, which apply equally to every member of the team, from his stars to the twelfth man on the bench.

John Wooden, arguably the greatest college basketball coach in history, would not allow star treatment on any of the teams he coached. Once Bill Walton, his all-American center, came to him objecting to the coach's rule on facial hair. Walton told Coach Wooden that he didn't think he should have to shave his beard because it didn't affect his play, and that it was a silly rule anyway. Coach Wooden didn't overreact. He calmly told his star that he admired a man of principle, a man who felt so strongly about his beliefs that he would give up his scholarship at UCLA rather than shave. Coach Wooden then wished Bill every success on his next college team. That stopped the star center in his tracks. At the next practice, he was clean-shaven.[3]

Vince Lombardi, the storied coach for the Green Bay Packers, had a similar reputation for fairness and consistency. As many of his stars fondly remembered, "He rode us all equally hard." In his pursuit of excellence, Coach Lombardi was totally colorblind. His system was based on merit alone. Only through hard work and effort did you become a starter for the Green Bay Packers. Every one of his players knew it, and loved him for it. Like John Wooden, Vince Lombardi's greatness can be measured by the vast number of players who continued to be influenced by him long after their careers were over—and even after the great coach's death. All of them would say that Coach Lombardi made them the men they are today.

Even Jesus of Nazareth had to deal with stars seeking special privileges. One night at supper, two of his apostles, James and John, cornered him to ask for the highest places of honor, seated on his right hand and on his left, when he went to his kingdom. Naturally, this created a furor among the other apostles who grumbled at James and John and their audacity to ask for such favoritism. But Jesus knew the damage this would do to "his team" and a sense of fairness among the twelve disciples. He merely counseled James and John, "If you wish to be great, seek the position of servitude first."[4]

THE ABUSE OF POWER

Perhaps there is no greater affront to fairness and consistency than the abuse of power. When people in high places or in positions of leadership get special treatment or fail to abide by the rules, it is an egregious betrayal of the public trust. Not surprisingly, it stirs up anger and animosity.

When Marie Antoinette said, "Let them eat cake!" in reply to, "Your majesty, they have no bread," it helped to ignite the French Revolution. Her aloof sense of privilege infuriated the common people. They soon exacted their revenge at the guillotine.

During our own Civil War, rich men could buy their way out of the draft. However, the poor were not able to escape conscription and the carnage of the war. In 1863, this gross inequity spawned the worst riots New York City had ever seen.

Richard Nixon tried to live by his own set of rules, above the law. The American public simply wouldn't stand for it. It finally took the Supreme Court to make him turn over the tapes that ultimately proved his complicity in the Watergate break in. Worse yet, the tapes revealed the "dirty tricks" he employed to circumvent the law and gain an unfair advantage in his re-election. As Nixon himself said, "The American public needs to know that their President is not a crook."[5] The nation soon discovered the irony of that statement. As the egregious disclosures became known, Nixon finally resigned rather than face certain impeachment.

Leona Helmsley was one of New York's richest women. She soon became known as the "Queen of Mean." The contempt she felt for common people was shown by her statement, "We don't pay taxes. Only the little people pay taxes."[6] She was later convicted of mail fraud and tax evasion. It was Helmsley's notoriously aloof manner in the courtroom that turned the jury against her. Americans have a low tolerance for arrogance and those who think they are above the law.

Power will always be dangerously intoxicating. Too often it can create a special class of people who think they are better than the rest of their countrymen. For example, our senators and representatives must always guard against passing laws that affect their fellow citizens, but insulate themselves from those very same edicts. Otherwise, they won't be able to relate to the problems ordinary citizens experience. Politicians who don't "share the pain" of the people they govern should not be allowed to pass laws affecting them.

As we saw with the Enron scandal, "white collar crime" can cost billions and is far more serious than petty theft. Yet, the chances of a rich man doing serious jail time are very slim because he can afford to hire an army of the best lawyers to defend him. Those expensive lawyers in their hand-tailored suits will drag out the legal proceedings, often for years. Even if the millionaire offender is finally incarcerated, it is likely to be in a "gentlemen's minimum-security prison." Where is the fairness in that? Their theft of billions often wipes out the life savings of thousands of ordinary workers. Their punishment should fit the crime, but it seldom does. It is this type of inconsistency that undermines the justice system.

Positions of authority carry with them increased responsibility. For example, judges, legislators, and law enforcement officers must hold themselves equally accountable to the laws that govern us all. When they don't, it undermines any sense of fairness in the system. Leaders must always be on guard against the temptations of power. As Lord Acton said so many centuries ago, "Power corrupts, and absolute power corrupts absolutely."[7]

FINAL THOUGHTS ON FAIRNESS AND CONSISTENCY

So what are the secrets of good leadership when it comes to fairness and consistency? Perhaps the first is: Abide by the rules yourself. There can be no favoritism on the team, especially for the boss. Sure, you may be eligible for head of the line privileges, but that doesn't mean you exercise that option.

Show you are willing to bear the burdens of the team's efforts, not just the fruits. There should be no job beneath your dignity, no danger that you won't share. During World War I, American General "Black Jack" Pershing was asked by a French general, "Why do your lieutenants lead the charge over the top from the trenches?" Pershing replied, "Because you can't push a string!"

Don't be afraid of showing fallibility. No one expects you to be perfect. In fact, they need to see your human side. Try to remedy inadvertent errors when you make them, but never attempt to cover them up.

Make all of your decisions for the common good of the team. In the Navy we have a judicial procedure called "Captain's Mast." During this formal hearing, the Commanding Officer serves as judge and jury for the accused.

Once, I was faced with a tough dilemma. The top performing helicopter aircrewman was brought before me after a random urinalysis uncovered an illegal drug in his system. This particular sailor was critical to our training effort because, at the time, he was the only enlisted aircrewman qualified in the squadron's new helicopter. His job was to teach, and then certify, the rest of the aircrewmen. If we discharged him from the Navy for drug abuse, it would set us back several weeks in our goal to reach operational readiness for the new squadron.[8]

Many of the other sailors in the squadron believed that we would abandon our tough anti-drug policy in order to keep this individual in the Navy. They expected him to get preferential treatment because his expertise was just too critical to the training effort to let him go. Understandably, all eyes were watching the outcome of this tough case because we had promised to discharge anyone caught for drug abuse. Everyone wondered if we would now bend the rules to save him.

We conducted the Captain's Mast in an open forum—so that anyone who wanted to could attend the proceeding. Everyone in the squadron was there, jammed into every corner of the ready room, and you could have heard a pin drop.

To the surprise of many, we discharged this sailor, even though he had once been our top aircrewman. But it was more important—for the "common good"—to have a consistent and fair drug policy than to keep this one man in the Navy. While it set us back in our training, it sent a powerful message that no one was above the law and no one would get special treatment, regardless of his status.

Also, by having everyone witness Captain's Mast, there could be no mistake about what had happened during the proceeding and whether it had been fair and impartial. Leadership should be

90 percent "carrot" and 10 percent "stick." Emphasize the positive, but let people know you will administer fair and impartial punishment, if that's what is called for.

Another important point: Always do what is right, regardless of the consequences. Once, as a young lieutenant, I was in charge of administering open and closed book written tests to my squadron—in the Navy we called it a Naval Air Training and Operating Procedures Standardization (NATOPS) exam. My Commanding Officer and Executive Officer asked me if it would be okay to take the exams in their offices instead of the squadron ready room with the rest of the pilots. I said that would be fine. However, about ten minutes later, as I was walking down the hall by their offices, I heard them hollering back and forth to each other, "Hey, what did you get for question #16?" They continued to share answers in this manner.

After the evaluation was completed, I had the uncomfortable task of going into the CO's office and telling him that his and the XO's written exams would not be counted in the squadron's test average. When he asked me, "Why not?" I told him the reason.

I knew full well that this was the man who would write my next fitness report, and a bad fitness report could end my career. But the integrity of the evaluation process was more important, and I was responsible for administering the NATOPS evaluation fairly to all squadrons in the Pacific, not just my own, regardless of the consequences.[9]

Any leader who wants to create an environment of fairness

and consistency must remember, if you promise something, do everything in your power to deliver it. Also, give credit to anyone making a contribution or offering an idea—especially if that idea is better than the one you originally had. It empowers them and also shows everyone that, just because you're the boss, doesn't make you the only one with good ideas. Look for the unsung heroes and make sure they get recognized. While it will be impossible to discover all of the remarkable things people are doing behind the scenes, especially on a great team, do your best to acknowledge as many as you find.

And finally, because it is so important, it bears repeating: Just as a good parent knows that all his children are different, so too does a good leader. Treating people differently might seem like a contradiction of the fairness principle. But no two people are alike, and therefore each person deserves to be treated in a unique and special way. Without question, it's the best way to unlock the untapped potential of each individual on your team.

REFLECTION AND DISCUSSION

1. Would you agree that consistency is a critical leadership trait? Explain.

2. Do you think that a different leadership approach for each individual violates the principle of fairness?

3. Give some of your own examples of poor leadership and the abuse of power.

4. Should "all stars" ever be given preferential treatment?

Chapter 11
Patience, Perseverance, and Adaptability

"I HAVE A DREAM THAT MY FOUR CHILDREN WILL ONE DAY LIVE
IN A NATION WHERE THEY WILL NOT BE JUDGED BY THE COLOR OF
THEIR SKIN BUT BY THE CONTENT OF THEIR CHARACTER."

MARTIN LUTHER KING, JR.

Becoming a better leader has much in common with learning to fly, learning the martial art of Aikido, or any other new skill. Often, progress comes in a series of breakthroughs, after weeks of seeming stagnation.

The human mind needs a gestation period to process, consolidate, and make sense of the many inputs it uses to create a unified whole. Like planting, fertilizing, and then harvesting, it's a process that can't be rushed or abbreviated. Learning follows those same patterns of nature. Improvement will happen when it happens. Don't be in a rush to get there overnight. Instead, enjoy the journey. Expect learning plateaus in anything new you attempt to master. But overall, when you look back, you'll be able to see the progress you've made.

Comparing yourself to others will only frustrate you. We all have our eureka moments at different times, unique for each individual. Trust that your daily effort toward improvement works if you can just be patient. Simply strive to be a little better than you were the day before. Realize that even during those seeming periods of stagnation or regression, learning, growth, and improvement are actually going on.

As a leader, are you able to see improvement as a natural process, one that takes time and patience? Or do you expect an immediate harvest, without tilling and planting the soil first? Are your decisions short sighted, governed by the tyranny of the quarterly report? Or are you able to think strategically with your focus on long-term goals? Do you take shortcuts just to look good now, but risk the long-term health of the company? Do you invest time developing your future leaders, or do you make all the decisions rather than take a chance that they'll make a mistake?

FIGHTING SPIRIT, GETTING UP OFF THE MAT

On October 29, 1941, Winston Churchill gave a speech at Harrow School in England. The crowd awaited his eloquent words with great anticipation. Finally, he rose to his feet, stepped up to the microphone and said, "Never give up; never give up; never give up."

Then he sat down.[1]

Those words summed up his whole approach to life. "The game is not over until the final whistle blows." It may sound trite, but think of the wisdom in that idea.

One of the greatest experiences in all of sports, or life for that matter, is the "come-from-behind" victory. Nothing is sweeter than defying the odds and winning when all hope is seemingly lost. But you will never experience that unbelievable exhilaration if you quit. The British endured the worst Hitler had to throw at them and came out victorious because they simply refused to give up.

What about your team? Do you teach them perseverance? Are they willing to fight on, no matter what? Has your team ever savored the come-from-behind victory, defying the odds? Remember, nothing is sweeter than the triumph over what was once thought impossible.

Failure doesn't matter. We all fail because we're all human. More important is what we do after being "thrown to the mat." That shows our true character.

We spoke of the British during the Second World War. They were swept off the beaches of Dunkirk, totally defeated. But their retreat wasn't the end. They regrouped to fight on in Africa, Sicily, and finally Europe, pushing the Nazis all the way back to Berlin.

The Chrysler Corporation was ready to declare bankruptcy in the 1980s. But Lee Iococca, the new president, led the company back from the brink of disaster by convincing his team to keep trying and not give up. They rededicated themselves to building quality automobiles at affordable prices. All employees agreed to wage concessions, and Lee Iococca himself received a mere $1.00 annual salary. He would receive other incentives, but only if the company succeeded. Chrysler defied the odds and made a complete recovery.[2]

How do you handle seeming defeat? Do you demonstrate tenacity, or give up early without a fight? Are you ready to defy the odds and prove the so-called experts wrong? Do you as a leader display a fighting spirit that permeates your entire team?

SEEK "MASA-KATSU-AGATSU"

"Masa-Katsu-Agatsu" means "True victory is victory over yourself." Many people spend an entire lifetime trying to control others: what they think, what they do, and what they say. It is a futile effort, guaranteeing only frustration. Your time is better spent working on yourself. Master yourself first, and then you can be a powerful influence on others.

How do you achieve self-mastery? Start by listing ten improvements you want to make in the next year. Every night, make an honest assessment of how you did that day. Don't beat yourself up. This self-appraisal must be detached and objective, free from blame or criticism. Approach it with the attitude of a scientist who merely remarks, "That's interesting."

Follow Benjamin Franklin's example by trying to make small,

incremental improvements every day. Over time, you'll be amazed. By harnessing your intent to change, together with an objective, daily self-appraisal, you'll begin to witness a transformation. In a sense, you start with a vision of the person you wish to become, and then slowly become that person.

It takes years of patience and painstaking effort, and a willingness to endure lapses and setbacks. But in the end, it will all be worth it because the direct benefactor is *you*. It's not easy, but it works. So persevere. Remember, Benjamin Franklin successfully used this method over an entire lifetime.

As a leader, do you waste time trying to change others but invest little time working on yourself? What's stopping you from beginning to change today? Is it because you expect instant results and don't have the patience? Or do you feel the road is too long to even begin? Just remember the ancient Chinese proverb, "The journey of one thousand miles begins with the first step."[3]

LOVE THEM ANYWAY

Throughout your life you will encounter people who betray you, talk behind your back, break promises, steal from you, envy you, belittle you, or turn their backs on your friendship. Love them anyway. This is probably one of the most difficult things to do. Most of us find it impossible.

It's easy to be nice to friends and people who treat us well. That's not much of a challenge. But to extend kindness to people who treat us badly takes remarkable spirit. Lincoln was vilified in the newspapers and by politicians who despised him. He was called an ape, sub-human, and worse. How did he respond? With self-deprecating humor, patience, and forbearance. He did not allow his enemies to bring him down to their level. Jesus Christ was totally innocent. But he was beaten, spat upon, scourged, and executed in the cruelest of ways, crucifixion. Yet, with his dying breath on the cross, he prayed that his enemies be forgiven, "Father, forgive them, for they know not what they do."[4]

How do you treat those who wish to hurt you? Do you have the strength of character to avoid descending to their level? Can you love them anyway?

LET FAILURE EMPOWER YOU

Sometimes it takes a two-by-four on the side of the head to wake us up. When we fail miserably, we realize the need to change. We finally admit that we've wandered into a blind alley and are going nowhere.

This awakening should be a call to action. Rather than being stunned by failure, get back on your feet and do something. Ask other members of your team to help you evaluate the situation. This is no time for yes men. Make an honest self-appraisal of what went wrong, and then fix it.

You may be surprised to discover that failure was just what was needed to energize your team and make necessary changes. While unpleasant at the time, it can be the "perfect medicine."

Are you devastated by failure, or do you let it empower you? It's okay to be knocked to the ground and lay immobile for a while. But eventually, you must get back on your feet, take stock of what happened, and get on with the recovery process.

BEN COMEN

Ben Comen is a remarkable young man. This sixteen-year-old student from Hanna High in Anderson, South Carolina, is the star of the cross-country team, but for reasons you might not expect. To tell you the truth, he has never won a race. But that doesn't stop him from trying. You see, Ben has cerebral palsy. He is a star because of his ability to inspire his teammates, fellow competitors, the townsfolk of Anderson—and now, an entire nation. His story has been featured in national magazines and television.

Ben never completes the race until long after everyone else has finished. But his teammates and competitors alike all return to the course to cheer him on. His tortured movements as he runs would never win style points, but his sheer determination and perseverance are something to behold. Ben falls often and hard, since his motor responses are too slow to reach out and cushion himself when he stumbles. But he never gives up.

"I've been coaching cross-country for thirty-one years," says Hanna's Chuck Parker, "and I've never met anyone with the drive that Ben has. I don't think there's an inch of that kid I haven't had to bandage up."

Sometimes people standing along the race course are brought to tears as they watch Ben's pluck and determination. Once, a collective gasp could be heard as they watched him crash to the ground fifteen yards from the finish line. But that didn't stop Ben. Struggling to his feet, he completed the race to thunderous applause.

For those who might ask why he does it, Ben has a ready answer, "Because I feel like I've been put here to set an example. Anybody can find something they can do—and do it well. I like to show people that you can either stop trying or you can pick yourself up and keep going. It's just more fun to keep going."

Ben is also a good student, builds homes for Habitat for Humanity and wheelchair ramps for Easter Seals, and spends nights helping at an assisted-living home. He is living proof that there are no limits on the human spirit when we persevere.[5]

"I HAVE A DREAM"

From the time they first set foot in the New World as slaves, African Americans have been engaged in a long struggle for dignity and equality. It took a bloody civil war and President Lincoln's courageous Emancipation Proclamation to end slavery. But even then their battle wasn't over. Blacks in America continued to endure racial bigotry and the ugliest side of man's nature. Secret white supremacist organizations such as the Ku Klux Klan and Jim Crow laws kept them from experiencing the American dream for many decades after the Civil War ended.

During the '50s and '60s, courageous civil rights leaders like Martin Luther King led patient, determined—but non-violent— protests and boycotts. Every night on their TV sets, Americans watched in horror as fellow citizens were knocked to the ground by fire hoses and attacked by police dogs. They saw the National Guard having to escort young black children to school through angry mobs screaming racial obscenities; they watched civil rights workers murdered and innocent worshipers die in bombings of black churches.

Finally, this injustice was too much for the American conscience to bear. New legislation was quickly passed giving these courageous citizens the rights they had been denied for so long. Their determined perseverance had won the victory.

While there was—and still is—much more work to be done, August 28, 1963, marked a turning point. Delivered on the steps at the Lincoln Memorial in Washington D.C., Martin Luther King's "I Have a Dream" speech still resonates for all Americans.[6] It calls on us to live up to the principles written in our Declaration of Independence and our Constitution.

THE SCREAMING EAGLES

It is often said "no battle plan survives first contact with the enemy." That doesn't mean that planning and preparation are a waste of time, only that you have to be able to adapt when circumstances change or new opportunities present themselves. This was certainly true in the early morning hours of D-Day, June 6, 1944, as the Screaming Eagles of the 101st Airborne Division prepared to parachute behind enemy lines at Normandy.

Due to heavy anti-aircraft fire, the C-47 transport planes flying them to their drop zones had to take wildly evasive maneuvers. This caused two very serious problems. First, the paratroopers were dropped as far as ten miles from their designated targets. Second, they were forced to bail out at a much lower altitude and a much higher airspeed. This higher speed literally ripped away the 100-pound supply and ammunition packs tethered below their feet as they bailed out. In fact, many paratroopers hit the ground without their rifles, ammunition, or critical supplies. The low altitude, high-speed bailout also resulted in more injuries.

So what did the Screaming Eagles of the 101st and their comrades in the 82nd Airborne do? They adapted. They used weapons, ammunition, and supplies from fallen comrades and enemy soldiers. Even though they were often separated from their parent units and widely scattered across the battlefield, they formed ad-hoc units among soldiers who had landed in the same drop zone. They engaged the Germans wherever they found them.[7] In fact, an Airborne Ranger knows beforehand that it is the nature of his mission to land in a drop zone already surrounded by the enemy. Adapting to the impossible is a key element of his arduous training, and this D-Day drop was nothing new in that regard.

Ironically, the fiasco of not getting to the correct drop zones ended up being a tactical coup. The Germans were utterly confounded by hordes of Allied paratroopers landing everywhere on the battlefield. They were unable to identify where the invaders were concentrated, and therefore failed to mount an effective counterattack. The American Rangers, even though lost and miles from their designated drop zones, didn't despair but adapted to the chaotic environment and defeated a confused German army.

How does your team adapt to chaos? Do they rise to meet the challenge? Do they regroup and fight on? Or do they collapse and disintegrate?

REFLECTION AND DISCUSSION

1. The civil rights movement in America is an enduring example of patience and perseverance. Can you think of others?

2. In your estimation, what historical figure best exemplified the traits of patience, perseverance, and adaptability?

3. The Screaming Eagles showed that they were able to adapt to difficult circumstances. What was your biggest challenge of handling the unexpected, and what did you learn from it?

4. Do you think America has become a culture of instant results and instant gratification? If so, how has that affected us as a nation?

Part III
The Golden Rule:
"Do Unto Others,
As You Would Have Them
Do Unto You"

Chapter 12
Servant Leadership

JOHN F. KENNEDY

The idea of servant leadership is certainly not a new concept.
But many leaders have forgotten how powerful it is and often
fail to use it, either through ignorance or arrogance.

Servant leadership actually goes back two thousand years. As
the Bible says: "The last shall be first, and the first last."[1] The idea
that leaders must put their people before themselves was a radical break with history up to that point. Before then, leaders ruled
through tyranny and fear. Life was brutal and cruel. Mercy was seldom seen. Conquered tribes—men, women, and children alike—
were put to the sword. No one was spared. Often a defeated army
was tortured and put to death in horrific ways. The Persians, then
the Greeks, devised crucifixion long before the practice was taken

up by conquering Roman armies.

Generals were equally brutal with their own soldiers. Discipline was harsh. Armies who failed in battle were "decimated." Literally, every tenth man in the defeated legion was executed.

Jesus Christ introduced a totally new philosophy to this brutish time in human history: servant leadership. He demonstrated this radical idea every day of his life. On the night before he was crucified, he showed once again what it meant to be a servant leader by washing the feet of his disciples before their last meal together. The apostle Peter protested, "Lord, it is I who should wash your feet." But Jesus replied, "Unless I wash you, you will have no inheritance with me." Peter responded, "Master, then not only my feet, but my hands and head as well."[2]

In today's world, as men and women climb the corporate ladder, they forget servant leadership. They often get caught up in their own self-importance. They begin to enjoy the perks of seniority. Worse yet, they come to expect them. Somehow leaders begin to think their own opinions are the only ones that matter since, obviously, they're the only ones who have achieved enlightenment. They easily dismiss the viewpoints of those supposedly less gifted and look to surround themselves with yes men who will reinforce the exalted opinion they already have of themselves and their own ideas.

This arrogance closes them off to the ideas of others, especially those junior to them. They think their way is the only way: "That's the way I did it; it worked for me." It becomes impossible to listen to new ideas. Consequently, subordinates always feel their heavy hand on the tiller and never get to steer for themselves.

On the other hand, servant leadership turns the corporate pyramid upside down. The more people who are junior to you, the more people you serve. That idea starts with the boss and must ripple down through every layer of management. It can't be faked; it must be real because people can sense the difference and will know immediately if it's just another management technique.

F. Terry Kremian of the Class of 1971 retired from the Marines following a successful twenty-plus-year career. He worked his way up the ladder in business as a director, vice-president, executive vice-president, chief operating officer, and eventually as president/ CEO of an acquired company. When asked about servant leadership he stated, "I do not believe in today's business world one can be a dictator or a micro-manager. To be effective you must serve those who look up to you for true leadership by providing a healthy and ethical environment but never losing sight of setting the example for others to follow. Encouraging individuals to be forthright and treating them with the utmost respect is a mark of a true servant leader."

So how do we become servant leaders? One method is to emulate great leaders from the past. History provides some amazing illustrations that we can use to inspire us.

THE STORY OF THE FOUR CHAPLAINS

On February 3, 1943, at 2:00 a.m., the U.S.A.T. *Dorchester* was torpedoed by a German U-boat in the freezing waters of the Atlantic Ocean. Four chaplains of four different faiths were aboard that fateful night: Rev. George L. Fox, Methodist, Rabbi Alexander D. Goode, Jewish, Rev. Clark V. Poling, Dutch Reformed Church, and Father John P. Washington, a Catholic priest. Each gave up his precious life jacket to another crewman.

Chaos reigned when the torpedo struck its devastating blow amidships. All lights and power went out. The four chaplains moved quickly about the ship trying to calm all hands. One young seaman approached Father Washington saying, "Padre, I have no life jacket, and I don't know how to swim." The good priest immediately gave up his own life jacket saying, "Here, take mine, son."

The chaplains directed men to the available lifeboats and restored calm and order aboard the doomed vessel. A sailor approached Rabbi Goode, "Rabbi, I have no gloves and my hands are cold." "Here, take mine," he replied.

On that fateful night, all four chaplains gave up their own life jackets and went down with the ship. They made the ultimate sacrifice and are credited with saving the lives of over 200 men.[3] Their example of servant leadership will never be forgotten.

JOHN F. KENNEDY

In his inaugural address of 1961, President John F. Kennedy established a new course for America with the inspiring words, "Ask not what your country can do for you; ask what you can do for your country."[4] In those few words, he defined servant leadership.

The United States has a long history of self-sacrifice. During the Revolutionary War, the British tried to flood the Colonies with counterfeit continental dollars. Their scheme was to undermine the fledgling nation's currency. By making American soldiers' pay worthless—"not worth a continental"—they felt certain Washington's army of volunteers would fall apart. Even Washington himself remarked, "A wagon full of dollars would not even buy a wagon full of supplies."[5]

But the British completely underestimated the American soldiers' willingness to put their new country first and risk their lives fighting the most formidable army in the world at that time. Even though their pay in continental dollars was virtually worthless, they accepted the promise it stood for. They endured frostbite and near starvation at their winter encampment at Valley Forge. And throughout the Revolutionary War, they were woefully outgunned, out-manned, and ill-equipped compared to the British regulars. But ultimately, their sacrifice and dedication to a cause above their own self-interest gave birth to a new nation.

Kennedy rekindled this spirit, inviting the youth of America to join the Peace Corps. He inspired Americans to return to their historical roots of service and self-sacrifice, once again putting their country first. He saw that as the key to lasting greatness. As Alexis de Tocqueville observed in the 1800s, "America is great because America is good; when she ceases being good, she will cease being great."[6] Servant leadership is a critical element of that goodness.

JESSE OWENS AND LUZ LONG

In both Olympic and world history, 1936 was a momentous year. Adolf Hitler was hosting the Games in Berlin, Germany, that year and wanted it to be a showcase for his concept of Aryan supremacy. There was only one problem with his theory, however: Jesse Owens.

Jesse was an American and the current world record holder in the long jump. The son of a sharecropper, Jesse had jumped 26 feet, 8 inches the previous year—amazingly, it was a record that would stand for twenty-five more years.

But Jesse was nervous as he watched Luz Long, the blond-haired, blue-eyed German warming up next to him. Luz was consistently hitting 26 feet in his practice jumps. And the political climate of "Aryan supremacy" put even more pressure on Owens. Clearly rattled, Jesse fouled in his first two attempts to qualify for the long jump finals. His distance was good but his take-off foot was hitting several inches beyond the foul line. If he missed again, he would be disqualified and have no chance for the gold medal.

It was then that Luz Long approached Owens. "Hey, you should have no trouble qualifying," he told Jesse. "You only have to make 23 feet 5 inches to be in the finals. Why don't you plant your take-off foot well behind the take-off board so that you don't risk another foul?"[7]

Owens followed his new friend's advice and qualified easily. He later beat Luz in the finals and won the gold medal in the long jump, one of four he would win in the 1936 Olympics. Hitler was furious. A black sharecropper's son had exploded the myth of Aryan supremacy.

Owens never saw Long again. He was killed in World War II. "You could melt down all the medals and cups I have," Owens later wrote, "and they wouldn't be a plating on the twenty-four-carat friendship I felt for Luz Long."[8]

Perhaps unknowingly, Luz Long taught the world a valuable lesson about servant leadership. Even though it may have cost him the Olympic gold medal, he put his friend Jesse Owens ahead of himself, something only a servant leader would do.

MOTHER TERESA OF CALCUTTA

Mother Teresa was born Agnes Gonxha Bojaxhiu in 1910 in Skopje, Yugoslavia. She joined the Sisters of Loreto in 1928 and took the name "Teresa" after St. Teresa of Lesiux, Patroness of the Missionaries.

In 1948, she came across a half-dead woman lying in front of a Calcutta hospital. She stayed with the woman until she died. From that point on, she dedicated the majority of her life to helping the poorest of the poor in India, thus gaining her the name "Saint of the Gutters." She founded an order of nuns called the Missionaries of Charity in Calcutta, India, dedicated to serving the poor. Almost fifty years later, the Missionaries of Charity have grown from twelve sisters in India to over 3,000 in 517 missions throughout

100 countries worldwide.[9]

In 1952, she founded the Nirmal Hriday Home for the Dying in a former temple in Calcutta. It was there that they would care for the dying Indians who were found on the streets. Mother Teresa would see Jesus in everyone that she met. It didn't matter whether they were dying of AIDS or leprosy. She wanted them to be able to die in peace and with dignity. For over fifty years, she worked unselfishly helping the poor. That devotion toward the poor won her respect throughout the world and the Nobel Peace Prize in 1979.

After a life of servant leadership, she died in 1997 at the age of 87.[10]

JIMMY CARTER

Jimmy Carter, a 1947 Naval Academy graduate, is the classic example of a servant leader. After reaching the pinnacle of power as the thirty-ninth President of the United States, he later worked as a common laborer for the Habitat for Humanity. Since leaving the presidency, he has swung his hammer in projects throughout the world, helping to build affordable housing for the less fortunate.

Jimmy Carter's involvement with Habitat for Humanity International began in 1984 when the former president led a work group to New York City to help renovate a six-story building with nineteen families in need of decent, affordable shelter. That experience planted the seed, and the Jimmy Carter Work Project has been an internationally recognized event ever since.

Each year, Jimmy and Rosalynn Carter give a week of their time—along with their building skills—to build homes and raise awareness of the critical need for affordable housing. The Jimmy Carter Work Project is held at a different location each year, and attracts volunteers from around the world.

"We have become small players in an exciting global effort to alleviate the curse of homelessness," Carter said. "With our many new friends, we have worked to raise funds, to publicize the good work of Habitat, to recruit other volunteers, to visit overseas projects, and even build a few houses."

Since leaving office, Carter has gained a reputation as a tireless champion for social justice. "Habitat has successfully removed the stigma of charity by substituting it with a sense of partnership," Carter said. "The people who will live in the homes work side-by-side with the volunteers, so they feel very much that they are on an equal level."[11]

This humble man and true servant leader won the Nobel Peace Prize in 2002 and the Naval Academy's Distinguished Graduate Award.

VIKTOR FRANKL

Perhaps no one better captures the concept of servant leadership than Dr. Viktor Frankl. Dr. Frankl was a Jewish psychiatrist from Austria, swept up in the horrors of the Nazi holocaust. Most of his family perished during those tragic years. But Viktor survived several death camps through his indomitable will—and as he tells it himself, luck.

It was from that experience that he gained his unique perspective, so beautifully expressed in his seminal work, *Man's Search for Meaning.*

Viktor Frankl tells us that man is the only animal that asks whether life has meaning. While animals follow instincts, man is intrinsically motivated by something much more profound. In fact, the true signature of being human is that man is outwardly directed to something other than self.

Dr. Frankl refers to this as "self-transcendence." We are drawn, by our very nature, to serve a cause or ideal greater than self. We are also called to live for others. In other words, when we truly love an ideal or another person, we are expressing the highest level of our humanity and truly fulfilling what it means to be human.

To illustrate this profound concept, Dr. Frankl uses the analogy of the human eye. Here are his own words:

In a way, your eyes are self-transcendent as well. Just notice that the capacity of the eye to perceive the surrounding world is ironically dependent on its incapacity to perceive itself, except in a mirror. At the moment my eye perceives something of itself, for instance a halo with colors around a light, it perceives its own glaucoma. At the moment I see clouding, I perceive my own cataract, something of my own eye. But the healthy eye, the normal eye, doesn't see anything of itself. The seeing capacity is impaired to the very extent to which the eye perceives something of itself.

It is the same with human existence. Human existence is distorted to the very extent one is primarily concerned with oneself, rather than letting happiness happen. People are striving for happiness by making it a target and thereby missing what they are aiming at.

Viktor Frankl was once asked, "What is the highest human achievement?" He replied that it was to master a very hard fate and then help others to master it as well. He told the story of a young man who was paralyzed from the neck down after a diving accident. Rather than wallow in self-pity, he went on to gain his degree in psychology. After that, using a stylus held between his teeth, he typed books written to help others with similar afflictions.[12]

That same higher calling could be applied to Viktor Frankl himself. Throughout his captivity in the death camps, he labored to console and encourage his fellow prisoners. By convincing them they had something to live for, he was able to save countless lives. He knew that prisoners who gave up hope would soon die. He wanted to give them a reason to live.

SOME FINAL THOUGHTS

Servant leadership is the highest expression of the human spirit. It makes us transcendent. We rise above our own self-interest and reach out to others. It is also an act of humility. We come to realize that we can't do it alone and that we need each other to succeed in this world.

We see servant leadership expressed in many ways. In historical accounts of human survival, we witness arctic explorers sharing their last scrap of food with more needy comrades, eating less themselves so that friends might survive.

In sports such as basketball, we watch a selfless point guard looking to pass the ball to his teammates first, before looking to score himself. To him, team success is more important than individual statistics. In football, we see huge linemen blocking for their running backs with no thought of personal accolades in tomorrow's sports headlines, but merely the pride in knowing they helped their team win. We watch pit crews at the Indianapolis 500, scrambling to shave precious seconds, knowing full well they'll never be seen taking the checkered flag.

Servant leadership becomes an expression of generosity. It does away with the "me first" mentality. On the best teams, it's a part of their culture, their only way of doing business. And when that happens, it resonates throughout the organization. Every team member becomes a servant to the others.

It is visible and tangible. Observers of the early Christians in the first century would remark, "See how they love one another." That spirit drew thousands of people to the early Christian church and fanned a blazing fire that spread across the whole Roman Empire.

Like the great rivers of the world, servant leaders place themselves below the streams that feed into them. They are generous with one of their most precious resources: time. They never look at the clock when counseling or interacting with their people. They offer continuous guidance and encouragement. They manage by walking around. They catch people doing a great job and acknowledge it immediately.

Servant leaders are good listeners. They find out their people's needs by asking them directly, then listening with genuine empathy. Most importantly, they act on what they've heard and give constant feedback.

Servant leaders mentor their people. They see it as a primary responsibility of leadership. They realize that everyone really wants to contribute and excel. Often, the only thing holding them back is the training and specialized knowledge they need to do a good job, so servant leaders ensure it is provided. They are also patient, understanding that every individual learns at his own rate.

We fondly remember the servant leaders we have known. They had profound impact on our lives and truly molded us and inspired us. They were our parents, coaches, teachers, friends, and bosses. Ultimately, we sensed their love for us and we returned it in kind.

Perhaps we've touched upon the simplest definition of servant leadership: love. Our goal then is to become servant leaders ourselves and to redirect that love to others. That will be our lasting legacy.

REFLECTION AND DISCUSSION

1. Who were some of the servant leaders who influenced you? Why?

2. List the character traits you think servant leaders should have.

3. In your opinion, who were history's greatest servant leaders?

4. Is servant leadership necessary for an organization to succeed?

Chapter 13
Humility

Ignore your press clippings. Don't build a "trophy case." As soon as you begin to bask in your own accomplishments, you start to become self-important. You start to think of yourself as better than others, someone deserving special treatment. You become aloof, unable to relate to others. This separation will lead to your downfall. You've now set yourself apart from the team. You've forgotten it was the team that got you where you are in the first place.

Remember, the talents that helped you succeed are only gifts anyway. They were never yours in the first place, just something on loan to you. They are meant to complement the gifts of others on your team. It doesn't make sense to boast about them or show off. Our goal should be to take this raw talent and develop it to the best of our ability. Nothing is sadder than seeing someone who has been blessed with great gifts waste them, or worse, use them to "lord it over" others.

In reality, deep down inside, we also know what our warts are. While we may try to hide these faults from others and pretend they don't exist, we can't wish them out of existence. When we're brutally honest with ourselves, we realize we have a lot to work on. There's much room for improvement.

Do you think you are perfect? Have you run out of things to improve upon? Then you haven't looked closely enough. That fact alone should keep us humble.

THE TROLL THAT SITS UNDER THE BRIDGE

Comedian Dennis Miller reminds us, "Ego is the troll that sits under the bridge."[1] He lurks there, waiting to ambush us. But we can learn an important lesson from the most influential men and women in history. Lincoln, Gandhi, Jesus, and Mother Teresa, to name just a few, all shared one important trait: humility. They preferred a place beside the common man. They never sought "privileged status" or "entitlement." Abraham Lincoln once said, "God must love the common man. He made so many of us."

Just as great rivers lie below the streams that feed into them, so do great men find their place as servant leaders. Their power and influence come from humility rather than pride. The Bible tells us that at the Final Judgment, "The first shall be last, and the last first." And it goes on to say, "Pride cometh before the fall."[2]

How about you? Is ego getting in your way? Have you lost touch with the other members of your team, thinking you're better than everyone else? Are you overly concerned with the perks of seniority, the big office, executive dining room, designated parking space, traveling first class?

DON'T SHOW OFF

It bears repeating: Our talents were meant to be used humbly, in the service of others. But sometimes it's tempting to "strut your stuff" and make a show of these gifts. However, when we do this, it's only because we've forgotten that our talents are on loan and were never really ours to begin with. And they certainly weren't meant to showcase us.

Sadly, however, we see many examples of the misuse of God-given talent. For example, we often observe running backs showboating in the end zone after a touchdown, taking off their helmets as they preen in front of the cameras; defensive linemen taunting the quarterback after a vicious sack; basketball players trash talking with an opponent up and down the floor.

Showing off is juvenile, arrogant, and totally lacking in sportsmanship. It is an abuse of talent and is merely a display of ego. It is better to follow the example of Navy's 1963 Heisman Trophy winner, Roger Staubach, one of the NFL's greatest quarterbacks. After a phenomenal play, he merely trotted over to the sideline as if nothing extraordinary had happened. You'd never know, from his body language, that he had just thrown or run for the winning touchdown.

How about you? Do you use your talents to help others, without fanfare? Or are you just showing off? We would all do well to remember what John Wooden, the great basketball coach from UCLA, said, "Talent is God-given; be humble. Fame is man-given; be grateful. Conceit is self-given; be careful."

NO ROOM FOR ARROGANCE

True leadership has no room for arrogance. It requires total honesty. When we see ourselves as we truly are, all arrogance should evaporate. We quickly see how flawed we are and how much work needs to be done.

Comparing ourselves to others is also a huge waste of time. There are two outcomes when we do this, both bad. We either become arrogant, thinking we're better than everyone else, or jealous, worried that we're not. Working on ourselves will take an entire lifetime. Trying to fix others is merely a distraction from that task.

If arrogance and self-importance still rule your life, keep these words from the Bible in mind, "Remember, man, thou art dust, and into dust thou shalt return."[3] You came into the world with nothing; you will leave with nothing.

EVEN OUR GREATEST HEROES HAVE WARTS

Many of the most beloved leaders in history were also very human. In fact, that's why we're able to connect with them so well. Leaders like Lincoln, Lee, and Gandhi are not remembered as perfect marble statues, but rather, real human beings with faults and failings like our own. However, they rose above their shortcomings to achieve greatness. Long after they died, they still serve as role models.

A true leader is "comfortable in his own skin." He knows exactly who he is, and therefore, has nothing to prove. This awareness of your own shortcomings allows you to be more tolerant of others. You stop looking for people to blame because you realize everyone falls short at some time or other. People sense your empathy and compassion. They know it's okay to fail, as long as they keep trying.

Great leaders never forget what it means to be human. They create an environment where saying, "I was wrong" or "I'm sorry," is perfectly acceptable. This unleashes a creative spirit that knows no limits. People no longer live in fear, constantly looking over their shoulders wondering what punishment might be meted out for a mistake. They dare to take risks.

Inspiring leaders laugh easily. They see the irony in the human condition and make light of overly serious situations. They give up the need to control everything—knowing it's an impossible task anyway. They are not obsessed with being in charge. Aware of their own shortcomings, they recognize more gifted members on the team and willingly step aside to play a supporting role. They know when to be the teacher, and when to be a student. By empowering others, they inspire the whole team. They follow the advice of Gandhi: "It is unwise to be too sure of one's own wisdom. It is healthy to be reminded that the strongest might weaken and the wisest might err."

Great leaders always know they are "a work in progress." They are humbled by their own ignorance, and therefore, constantly seek new growth and learning. They recognize that knowledge can come from any source, not necessarily the so-called experts or senior members of the team. Inspiring leaders are not afraid to be rookies when operating outside their area of expertise. They are willing to admit, "I don't know," and begin learning. They set an example for others to do the same. A wise man once said, "If you do not take the time to sit at the feet of someone who has talents and knowledge you do not possess, then they will be lost forever."

Conscience drives all of their decisions. They listen to that brutally honest voice within to keep them humble. They do what is right, even when it may not make them wealthy or popular.

They follow Helen Keller's advice: "I long to accomplish great and noble tasks, but it is my chief duty to accomplish humble tasks as though they were great and noble. The world is moved along, not only by the mighty shoves of its heroes, but also by the aggregate of the tiny pushes of each honest worker."[4]

In the end, humble leaders know that the words of James M. Barrie are true: "Life is a long lesson in humility."

THE POWER OF MISTAKES

Learning the value of making mistakes will keep us humble and release our creativity. All of us spend far too much time and energy worrying about mistakes and looking bad. But in truth, none of mankind's greatest achievements was ever realized without a lot of mistakes being made along the way.

Think about it: The whole history of aviation is filled with failures. Some of our earliest rockets crashed and burned on the launch pad. Many test pilots and astronauts were killed as we pushed back the frontiers of space.

Even our own experience of learning to ride a two-wheeled bike was accomplished only after numerous falls. If you did it the hard way, without training wheels, you probably scraped most of the paint off your new bike before you mastered this skill. Would you have ever guessed that learning was going on as you fell time and time again? But it was! Your subconscious mind was making adjustments after every uncoordinated spill. A wise man once said, "Take note of where you stumble; that's where the treasure lies." Our greatest accomplishments often occur after seeming failures.

Thomas Edison tried ten thousand different materials for the filament of the electric light, all of them abject failures. When he was asked, "Mr. Edison, you're no better off than when you started. What have you learned?" He replied, "Well, now I know ten thousand things that don't work."[5] That's the right attitude about making mistakes!

An insightful man said, "I try to make as many mistakes as fast as I can, because that way I'll learn more quickly." Practice was never meant to be perfect. It was meant to be a time for making mistakes and learning. After all, what is a flight instructor but a safety pilot who is there to let his student make mistakes in a safe environment?

The pursuit of perfection is neurotic; the pursuit of excellence, however, is a worthy goal. The only tragedy in making a mistake is not learning something from it. Mistakes are inevitable and, more important, vital to growth and learning. We would all have a lot less anxiety in our lives if we kept this in mind.

As a leader, it's very important how you respond to mistakes, both your own and those of the people you lead. When you yourself do something really stupid, do you try to cover it up or blame a subordinate? If you do, then the message you are sending is that "I'm perfect and above making mistakes"—they already know you're not, so you've lost credibility as well—and that mistakes should be covered up rather than exposed to scrutiny or embarrassment. In other words, nobody should ever tell the emperor that he doesn't have on any clothes. But that's disastrous for an organization.

If one of your subordinates makes a mistake, do they land in your personal doghouse? How likely are they to ever experiment with something new or risky in the future? Remember that improvement requires change, change requires experimentation with new ideas, experimentation inevitably means mistakes, but mistakes lead to learning and progress. A turtle moves ahead only when he sticks his neck out. Otherwise, he's just a stationary rock.

Have you ever watched a sword smith at work? He takes the rough and imperfect metal and heats it in the furnace. Then he pulls it out of the fire and pounds on it with a hammer to temper and harden it. Back into the furnace it goes. After a few minutes, it's taken out and hammered again. This process is repeated hundreds of times until all the imperfections in the metal are pounded out. Only then has he created a sword worthy of his stamp on the blade.

In a sense, we are all like that sword. We make our mistakes and must be put back in the furnace, then hammered to remove our imperfections. This process is repeated until the lesson is finally learned. Over time, after many mistakes, we become better human beings. That's the lesson of the sword.

The best thing you can do for your organization is to cultivate a healthy attitude about making honest mistakes. If you treat them as learning opportunities and necessary for progress, you will have taken a giant step in driving out fear from your team. Accountability still remains, but your culture will shift from one of blaming to one of learning. In the end, when mistakes are made, the only thing that will matter is, "Did you learn something?"

As John J. McCloy tells us, "Humility leads to strength and not to weakness. It is the highest form of self-respect to admit mistakes and to make amends for them."

HUMILITY'S EFFECT ON A TEAM

As we examine humility's effect more closely, we see how it totally liberates the creative energies of the team. Fear is driven out. People dare to try a fresh approach. Mistakes are seen as healthy byproducts of experimentation.

A sense of camaraderie takes over. The team becomes far more important than individual accomplishments and one-upsmanship. Status and perks no longer matter. Team success does.

In contrast, when the goal is merely to assemble a team of "all stars," we often find a bunch of greedy prima donnas, fighting for the spotlight. We've all witnessed sports teams where each member is looking to "pad his own stats" at the expense of the team so that he can ask for a fatter contract the next time it comes up for renewal. A "lesser team" who work unselfishly for each other easily beats this assemblage of inflated egos.

Isn't it also interesting how success can breed arrogance and complacency? Samuel Tilden tells us, "Success is a ruthless competitor, for it flatters and nourishes our weaknesses and lulls us into complacency. We bask in the sunshine of accomplishment and lose the spirit of humility, which helps us visualize all the factors that have contributed to our success. We are apt to forget that we are only one of a team, that in unity there is strength and that we are strong only as long as each unit in our organization functions with precision."

We saw what happened to the American auto industry many years ago when their attitude was, "Hey, if we build them, they'll buy them." It took the Japanese, with an interest in discovering what customers really wanted, to teach us a valuable lesson in humility. Hubris nearly destroyed the American auto industry!

HUMBLE LEADERS SHARE THE RISKS

Great leaders never put themselves above those they lead. Rather, they stand shoulder to shoulder with them.

In 480 B.C., King Leonidas led his three hundred Spartans against the invading Persians and their king, Xerxes. Vastly outnumbered and facing certain death, this tiny band of brave warriors held off thousands of enemy Persians at the narrow pass of Thermopylae. They were defeated only when a fellow Greek betrayed them. This traitor showed the Persians a secret pass behind the Spartans' defensive position. As a result, the Spartans and their warrior king were outflanked, surrounded, and slaughtered, but only after three days of fierce, hand-to-hand fighting.

In contrast to the leadership of Leonidas, it is interesting to note that King Xerxes chose to watch the entire battle from his golden throne on a hillside well above the fray. From this safe position, he ordered wave after wave of Persian soldiers against the Spartans.

Although King Leonidas and his men were finally defeated by a treacherous betrayal, their bravery inspired all of Greece. Xerxes and his invaders were eventually defeated and forced to retreat to Persia, never to threaten Greece again.[6] Even today, the brave stand of the three hundred Spartans at Thermopylae lives on in our memories and will never be forgotten.

Like Leonidas, the Scotsman William Wallace was noted for fighting alongside his men in the front lines against the English, sharing the dangers and hardships of battle with them. It is no wonder they revered him.

General Robert E. Lee was noted for courage his entire military career. Although his army was usually outnumbered during the battles of the Civil War, he often rode his horse, Traveler, into the thick of the fight to inspire his men whenever the outcome was in doubt. But he was so highly regarded by his soldiers that they quickly ushered him to safety with the cry, "Lee to the rear, Lee to the rear," lest their beloved leader be lost.[7]

During the Civil War in the campaign to seize Norfolk, Abraham Lincoln personally scouted the coastline to let his troops know the best place to come ashore, an unprecedented risk for the Commander-in-Chief.

Chesty Puller, the Marine Corps' most highly decorated officer, always pitched his command tent near the front lines. His willingness to share the dangers of battle inspired his men, and his example of bravery amidst the carnage often gave his beloved Marines the margin of victory.[8]

All of these leaders from history followed the advice of the ancient Chinese philosopher Lao-Tzu: "Avoid putting yourself before others, and you can become a leader among men." He went on to say, "Be humble and you will remain entire. The sages do not display themselves; therefore they shine. They do not approve themselves; therefore, they are noted. They do not praise themselves; therefore they have merit. They do not glory in themselves; therefore they excel."

REFLECTION AND DISCUSSION

1. Would you agree that humility is a sign of strength rather than weakness in a leader?

2. Which leaders in history had true humility?

3. Do you think it is wise for leaders to expose their shortcomings to those they intend to lead?

4. In what ways can a leader demonstrate humility?

Chapter 14
Example

When it comes to discussions about leadership, much is said about example. What role does it really play? Simply this: Leadership is 100 percent example, period! Everything we learn about leadership comes from watching leaders in *action*. Words are far less important. In fact, we really don't care much about what leaders say if their words don't match their actions.

Think back. We get our first cues from our parents. Like dry sponges, we soak up everything we observe about them: their mannerisms, speech patterns, behavior, how they discipline, and so forth. The same is true about how we learn leadership. Our own style becomes a composite of what we've learned by watching other leaders. And make no mistake about it, we learn from bad leadership as well as good. Hopefully, we decide never to treat other people the way that poor leaders once treated us.

Leaders often don't realize how closely they are scrutinized. But subordinates pick up on everything, and actions have the strongest impact. If you don't think this is true, attend a going away party for someone in a leadership position and watch the skits and other humorous parting remarks that are made. You'll often find a hilarious parody of all the leader's peccadilloes.

For many of the graduates from the Class of 1971, choosing the right role model was a key element in their own development as leaders. Leadership by example became the foundation for their careers. In many instances, the leaders they chose will come as no surprise to us. Lee Burgess, a successful small business owner and no stranger to leadership positions such as president/CEO/vice-president, and senior partner, believes that leading by example is his number-one value when it comes to leadership. He has experienced leaders who paved the way for him, and like most other respondents to our leadership survey, chose one of his Commanding Officers from his early Navy days as a role model. "He was fair-minded, patient with naïve ensigns like me, led purely by example, and treated every single person with respect and dignity," Lee stated. "Moreover," he added, "one of my first bosses in the business world was a superior example of not asking anyone to do anything that he wouldn't do himself. Both these leaders were exemplary in their projection of true leadership and have stuck with me for my entire professional life."

Retired Captain Greg Harper, a professor of leadership and ethics at the Naval Academy and Class of 1971 graduate, considered retired Army General Colin Powell, and current Secretary of State, to be the epitome of leadership by example. Many of our respondents felt that General Powell and President Reagan were two leaders who never equivocated on their principles and values. Classmate Mike James, CEO of a consulting firm and former executive with KPMG and SPRINT, considered retired Vice Admiral James Stockdale a national treasure for his steadfast loyalty to his fellow POWs and the example he set every single day while held captive in Vietnam. Another classmate, Steve Dmetruk, considered Jack Welch, GE's highly successful CEO, not only one of the most ethical leaders in the business world but also one who truly set the standard of excellence and the example for others to follow. All of these role models, whether they are military, government, or private industry leaders, demonstrated through their actions a clear and distinct message to those who followed them.

As a leader, what message are you sending? Are you more concerned with your position and privileges than the welfare of your people? Do you pitch in when they need help, or are you a prima donna? There should be no job beneath your dignity. When people know that, it gives you great power as a leader. Set the example and lead by your actions.

MAJOR "JOE" HENDERSON

Major Lofton R. "Joe" Henderson, Naval Academy Class of 1926, was assigned as a Squadron Commander with Marine Air Group 22 located on Midway at the start of World War II. His squadron consisted of sixteen new "Dauntless" dive-bombers and fourteen old "Vindicators." The majority of his pilots were either experienced aviators, who were unfortunately unfamiliar with the Dauntless, or were "nuggets" (fledgling aviators) who had not yet worked together and were still learning the basics of operational flying.

For a month and a half, Major Henderson worked night and day to prepare his Marines and their airplanes for the upcoming fight. On the eve of the battle, he assessed his unit's capability. Because many of his aircraft were so inferior and the vast majority of his pilots were so new, he saw the situation as a "one way trip." He passed the word that the mission he expected in the morning would be strictly voluntary. He announced that he would be taking off as soon as the Japanese fleet was in range—the other pilots could follow if they wished.

About 0550 on June 4, 1942, word reached Midway that the Japanese fleet had been spotted by one of its patrol planes. Immediately all the flyable planes were launched. As the last unit in line to take off, Henderson's squadron launched in two sections with the lead aircraft of the Japanese air raid only forty miles away—no time to brief or coordinate, they had to just GO!

Following Major Henderson's example, every one of his pilots volunteered to fly that day. Within twenty minutes, every plane that could fly was airborne. Only three of the sixteen pilots in Henderson's section had any experience flying Dauntlesses, and ten of them had been in the squadron barely a week. They didn't know each other well, and had virtually no time to train together.

Because of this lack of experience and proficiency, Henderson had decided to abandon the more effective but difficult dive bombing attack for simpler glide bombing. The plan was simple: Follow the leader! This left them much more vulnerable to anti-aircraft fire and fighters, but proved more effective in the long run.

About 0755, they spotted the Japanese fleet, steaming about 160 miles northwest of the island. Immediately Major Henderson signaled for an attack and began a wide turn in toward the Japanese carrier, *Akagi*. Anti-aircraft fire and then Japanese fighters quickly hit him, and with his wings burning, he crashed in the sea near the ship. However, the rest of his section and squadron pressed home their attack with bombing and strafing, completely disrupting the Japanese fleet.

The combined attack of the Dauntlesses and Vindicators lasted only fifteen minutes, yet it had a powerful impact on the battle. Just as the last Marine bombers were being driven away, the Japanese spotted our fleet. Because of Henderson's attack, there was nearly an hour delay before the enemy could even begin preparing for a second attack.

This hour proved to be one of the most critical in the war. Henderson's attack had forced the Japanese to launch extra defensive fighters, delayed the recovery of the Japanese planes returning from the strike on Midway, and had caused the carriers to break formation and spread far apart. This prevented the Japanese from initiating a second strike and started a chain of events, which resulted in the Japanese carriers being caught with full decks two hours later.

Midway was a battle decided in a matter of a few minutes, and it is no exaggeration to say that Major Joe Henderson's raw courage and example played a critical part in the way it turned out.

We may never know the implications of our daily actions. Major Henderson could not predict the consequences of his example, and, unfortunately, did not live to see them either.[1]

GENERAL JIM GAVIN

June 6, 1944, was only a few hours old, and things were going badly for the men of 1st Battalion, who had parachuted into a buzz saw. The three senior leaders were dead, and German artillery pounded the GIs as they hacked foxholes in the Norman soil. In the distance, they heard every foot soldier's worst nightmare: enemy tanks on the move.

Twenty-four-year-old Lieutenant Dean McCandless was in the

battalion command post, a fancy name for a couple of shallow holes alongside an important road. McCandless saw a GI approaching, walking upright through the heavy fire. "Get down!" he screamed. The soldier pressed on stubbornly, until a stunned McCandless realized it was General Jim Gavin.

Gavin surveyed the area, hot with flying shrapnel. Badly wounded men were being carried to the dubious safety of an aid station. But there was no safe rear area, no evacuation route. The paratroopers were—as always—surrounded. "I was thinking about moving the command post," McCandless told the general as artillery crashed around them.

"Nah, we're holding our own," Gavin said, as calmly as if talking about a training exercise. "We're in place, where we're supposed to be, so we should stick around."

"Besides," he said, grinning, "there's no place else to go."

With those few gestures—his walk to the command post, his calm assessment of a dire situation, even his smile—Jim Gavin did what a leader is supposed to do in tough circumstances: He shared his confidence and he inspired those around him. For McCandless, the general's presence was a tonic. The soldiers had learned to trust Gavin over the previous two years and two campaigns. He made them believe they would hold, and they did.

The leadership lessons of 1944 are still valid today. The personal connections a leader establishes are critical; personal example is everything.[2]

GENERAL CHARLES C. KRULAK

General Charles C. Krulak, the former Commandant of the Marine Corps, had this to say about the power of example:

"The concept of leadership by example is alien to many in our society today, but it is central to who we are. For those of us who belong to the profession of arms, whether we serve on land, in the air, on or below the sea, this concept is the bedrock of our philosophy. It is just as important in peacetime as it is in times of war. It is just as important in the junior ranks as it is in the senior ranks. It is just as important off duty as it is on duty. And it is just as important out in town as it is on base. You cannot lead by memo, you can not lead by shouting, you can not lead by delegation of your responsibility. You must lead by example.

"Marines and sailors are going to remember your example. Are you ready to lead by example? Consider the following: What happens when you eat, sleep, or go on liberty before the troops do? You fail to report an error or mistake? Your uniform is unkempt? You lose your temper? You bounce a check? You return a salute in a sloppy manner? You go out on a date with someone who is married? Your marines or sailors receive punishment because they modeled your negative example?

"Imagine the difference between those negative examples and the following: You go to the back gate on Christmas Day and wish the sentries Merry Christmas and thank them for protecting the base on a holiday. You research the background of a different member of your unit every day and sometime while on duty talk to them about the weather back home, how their sports team is doing, or some bit of local news. You put on overalls and go down to the motor pool and change the oil on the unit vehicles with your mechanics. You walk shoulder to shoulder with your troops as they conduct the morning FOD walk, picking up foreign objects and debris from the flightline. You visit someone from your unit in the hospital and bring them a book or magazine. You are the first one at work in the morning and the last one to leave. You get to work early and watch your unit hold reveille.

"You are always where you are supposed to be, before you are supposed to be there, in the right uniform, and prepared for the mission. The list could go on and on. The point is, when all eyes are on you—and all eyes will always be on you—your example will be the measure of your leadership. Leadership by example is the bedrock of our profession. Whether you want it to or not, your example will have an enormous impact and influence on the Naval Services. Never underestimate its importance."[3]

SIR ERNEST SHACKLETON

Sir Ernest Shackleton showed us how powerful a leader's example can be. Shackleton led twenty-seven men during the "Heroic Age of Exploration" aboard the *Endurance* in a valiant attempt to reach the South Pole. In recruiting men for his 1914–1916 Antarctic expedition, Shackleton posted the following notice:

MEN WANTED FOR HAZARDOUS JOURNEY. SMALL WAGES. BITTER COLD. LONG MONTHS OF COMPLETE DARKNESS. CONSTANT DANGER. SAFE RETURN DOUBTFUL. HONOR AND RECOGNITION IN CASE OF SUCCESS.

The *Endurance* later became trapped in polar ice. Shackleton knew there was no hope of extricating the ship from the lethal grip of the ice, but he allowed his men to chip away with shovels, saws, and pickaxes so that they could see for themselves that it was futile. Shackleton knew they would ultimately have to abandon the *Endurance*, but he wanted no second-guessing of his decision when he finally had to give the order.

As shifting sea ice slowly crushed the wooden hull, breaking it into splinters, Shackleton displayed no sign of despair. He simply and calmly told his men that they would have to spend the winter on the pack ice. Their highly respected leader, whom they called "The Boss," would lead them by his personal example, both physically and emotionally. Shackleton always put his men's welfare before his own.

During their long, two-year ordeal in the frozen hell of the Antarctic, they could always look to Sir Ernest for inspiration when morale began to sag. He kept them busy with football games, nightly sing-alongs, and dog sled races. In humorous solidarity, they all shaved their heads, posing for expedition photographer, Frank Hurley. Shackleton knew that maintaining high esprit de corps was the only way to survive. He taught all of his men to pull together.

Shackleton's humanity was also infectious. He was a true servant leader. Rising early every morning, he hand-delivered hot milk to each tent in the camp. His men took notice and were inspired by his example. Once, when First Officer Lionel Greenstreet spilled his precious ration of hot milk, he seemed despondent over his loss. Without a word, the other seven men in his tent willingly poured some of theirs into his cup, refilling it.

Shackleton would not allow special treatment for himself or other high-ranking officers. Senior scientists scrubbed decks alongside the most junior seamen. University professors ate with Yorkshire fishermen. When it came time to cast lots for the warmest, fur-lined sleeping bags, invariably Shackleton and his officers ended up with the old, wool bags. This odd coincidence did not go unnoticed by the junior sailors. They knew the outcome had been manipulated by "The Boss" to make sure they were taken care of first.

Knowing they were doomed if they stayed on the Antarctic pack ice, Shackleton inspired his men to head out across the trackless southern ocean in their open lifeboats. After seven days at sea, they finally reached Elephant Island, where the majority of Shackleton's men encamped. Not long afterward, Shackleton and five others set sail once again, this time for South Georgia Island. Their destination was a small whaling village, the only civilization for thousands of miles. He knew if he failed to make contact with the outside world and get help, all of his men back on Elephant Island would soon perish.

The daunting trip to South Georgia Island took seventeen days! Hour after hour, Shackleton stood at the tiller, sailing into the teeth of gale force winds. Whenever he would notice one of the men cold and shivering, he immediately ordered another hot drink served to all. Shackleton did not want to single out the man suffering most or make him fearful about his deteriorating condition.

Amazingly, Shackleton and his men made it to South Georgia Island, but their ordeal was not over. The whaling village they needed to reach was on the other side of the island, and their route was blocked by a jagged, snow-covered mountain range. In spite of all they had suffered, Shackleton and two of his men set out once again, this time to cross the rugged peaks. Calling upon their last reserves of strength, they made it over the summit and descended to the village below. Upon seeing Shackleton and his two companions, the whaling men were shocked at their ravaged faces, but even more astounded by their extraordinary tale of seamanship.

Ultimately, all of Shackleton's men were rescued. His inspiring leadership and personal example had saved them all. Never once did they doubt that their selfless leader would return for them. In the face of the most daunting challenges and constant danger, Shackleton remained courageous, positive, and decisive, keeping his men's morale high. He brought out the best in each of them and enabled them to endure nearly two years of unimaginable hardship. To this day, Shackleton is remembered as one of the greatest leaders of the Heroic Age of Exploration.[4]

JESUS OF NAZARETH

No figure in history had more impact than Jesus Christ. This humble man from a small, conquered nation on the fringes of the Roman Empire came to influence the world like no other, before or since.

Jesus taught us in the most powerful way, by his example! "Learn of me," he said, "because I am meek and humble of heart: and you shall find rest to your souls."[5]

His example was a startling contrast to accepted leadership practices of the time. Mercy—especially to one's enemies!—was unheard of. Gentleness was thought to be a sign of weakness. At that time in human history, instilling fear was the only way to exercise control. Most of the known world lived under the boot of the Imperial Roman Army and the Emperor, Caesar Augustas. Any nations who rose up against the empire were slaughtered without mercy. Brutality was an accepted way of life. Only an elite few lived in luxury—and always at the expense of the vast majority who scratched out a meager existence in unremitting poverty.

Jesus chose to come into this world, not as one of the privileged, but as the poorest of the poor, born in a shepherd's cave. He grew up in a small, backwater town called Nazareth, a lowly carpenter's son. But from these humble origins, the way he lived his life gave an example for the entire world to follow.

Early in his ministry, he taught us to revere the innocence and openness of children. No matter how tired Jesus was, he always had time for them, telling his disciples, "Do not send them away; let the little children come to me." He taught his followers, "Unless you are like these children, you shall not enter the Kingdom of Heaven."[6]

Jesus felt so strongly about the power of bad example that he once said, "But who so shall offend one of these little ones which believe in me, it were better for him that a millstone were hanged about his neck, and that he were drowned in the depth of the sea."[7]

Jesus chose the company of sinners and the down and out. When challenged by the privileged Jewish elite about the company he was keeping, he simply replied, "It is the sick who have need of a doctor, not those who are well."[8]

Jesus taught humility and servant leadership by washing the feet of his disciples before their last meal together. When told of the death of his good friend, Lazarus, his compassion was visible. The shortest sentence in the Bible tells us simply, "Jesus wept."[9]

But Jesus was by no means a pushover. He fearlessly confronted the arrogant and the powerful, calling them "hypocrites and a brood of vipers." He showed righteous indignation when he saw the moneychangers desecrating the holy Temple of Jerusalem, "his Father's house." They scattered like vermin as he upended their tables and chased away this "den of thieves."[10]

But the most important example Jesus gave us was his love. He knew that people were starving for a message of hope in their oppressive lives. He came on Earth to tell us the "good news" of a heavenly Father and his infinite love for us. He told the people, "Come to me all you who are heavily burdened, and I will give you rest."[11]

In fact, Jesus' every action was a demonstration of love. He showed us by his example how to be kind, generous, and forgiving. On the eve of his death, he said to his followers, "Love one another, as I have loved you." Ultimately, Jesus made the supreme gesture of love by dying for us on a cross. "Greater love hath no man than this, that he lay down his life for his friends."[12]

His example is unmatched in history and gave hope to all of mankind. It is a brilliant light so powerful that it can never be extinguished.

REFLECTION AND DISCUSSION

1. Do you consider example to be one of the most powerful leadership tools?

2. In what ways are you influenced by a leader's personal example?

3. Which leaders serve as your personal role models? Why?

4. Is it possible for a leader to be effective without being a role model?

Chapter 15
Love and Friendship

"GREATER LOVE HATH NO MAN THAN THIS, THAT HE LAY DOWN
HIS LIFE FOR HIS FRIENDS."

JOHN 15:13

Too many organizations overlook the value of friendship. Workers are expected to arrive on time, punch the clock, and work at peak efficiency all day. They have set time limits for coffee breaks and lunch. And woe to those employees who dare linger around the coffee pot for an extra minute sharing stories about their families and building friendships. They are not logging "billable hours" and are wasting company time. Sound familiar?

This sort of corporate thinking is misguided. To show you why, we must return to World War II and the U.S. Marines on Guadalcanal. On that bleak island back in 1942, our Marines were engaged in some of the most horrific fighting of the war: vicious hand to hand combat, suicidal banzai charges, malaria, limited supplies and ammunition. Their situation was so desperate that they weren't even expected to survive. The Navy was faced with the prospect of imminent defeat and retreat to New Guinea as the Marines were swept off the island.

Somehow, for some reason that defied explanation, the Marines were able to hang on and win the battle of Guadalcanal. No one could figure out why until they asked the individual Marines. Here is what each of them said: "I didn't want to let my buddy down in the next fox hole. If he was willing to fight on, so was I."[1]

What a powerful statement about friendship. And what a lesson that is for any team. When you forget about friendship, you lose the mortar that holds the bricks together. If employees are just machines putting in their time, punching the clock, and going home, they're not making those personal connections necessary for high morale and a winning organization. They have no stake in each other's success. That comes only from strong friendships. When leadership doesn't allow members to interact on a personal level, that team will fail.

While allowing employees to linger for a few minutes around the coffee pot may seem inefficient, it is one of the best intangible investments you can make. Friendships are being built. And ultimately, friendship is why people pull together for the good of the team.

So why does friendship have such impact? Because true friends really know each other well. They go the extra mile. They're good listeners and are willing to overlook faults. They have empathy and anticipate each other's needs. This cooperative environment makes work flow smoothly. When talking on the phone, don't we always feel more comfortable when the person on the other end is a friend rather than a perfect stranger? To understand the importance of friendship, just imagine a team without it.

WINNING TEAMS

Mickey Mantle, the great Hall of Fame center fielder for the New York Yankees, used to say that he could identify a winning team, even if he was unfamiliar with the sport, simply by observing the players' behavior in the locker room after a game. What do you think he saw in the team with a losing record?

You probably guessed it: lots of "sniping" among the players, the defense complaining that the offense couldn't put enough points on the board, or the offense complaining that the defense couldn't hold them, or perhaps complaints about the way the special teams played. Lots of blame being spread around. Or maybe the locker room was as quiet as a tomb.

On the other hand, in a winning locker room, Mickey would observe just the opposite: lots of back slapping, praise, appreciation for each other, and laughter. Generally, a very upbeat atmosphere with evidence of strong friendships everywhere you looked. Anyone who has played organized sports knows exactly what Mickey was talking about.[2]

Lou Holtz, the great head football coach at Notre Dame for many years, assembled his players before the first spring practice of 1988. At that meeting, he asked the players to make a pact: *They would never say anything negative about a teammate the entire year.* And you know what happened? Those players kept that promise to each other, and Notre Dame won the national championship. It's a powerful statement about the positive energy that results when teammates are friends who support each other and avoid a negative attitude, isn't it?

Today we see the symptoms of a lack of friendship: zero loyalty and no sense of teamwork. Without true camaraderie, we have layoffs, "virtual companies," and athletes who sell their talents to the highest bidder. Lee Iacocca fought this in the 1980s and was able to turn things around at Chrysler by establishing a common purpose, making everyone realize that they would either sink or swim together.

How are things in your organization? Do "snipers" roam freely? Is there a lot of backbiting? Jealousy? Do people pull together or tear one another apart? Are departmental feuds common? Or is there a sense that everyone is in this together? Do people go that extra mile to help each other out? Is there a strong sense of camaraderie? Laughter? Friendship?

Would Mickey Mantle have described your "locker room" as a winning one? If not, what are you doing as a leader to change things?

YOU'RE NEVER ALONE

I strongly suspect that those who commit suicide have given in to total despair. They must feel terribly alone and without hope at the moment they take their own lives.

But every person walking the face of this Earth is important. The loss of any one of us diminishes us all. Where there is life, there is always hope. Even the most despicable of men can turn his life around and become a force for good. The Bible tells us about Saul, on his way to Damascus to kill Christians. He was struck from his horse and became Saint Paul, one of Christianity's greatest saints.

I'm convinced that Jesus mourned the death of his betrayer, Judas. Even if a man seemingly has no friends, there is a Higher Power who cares for him. That, in itself, is reason enough never to give up hope.

Do you ever give in to despair or a sense of abandonment? Is there someone you know who appears to have done so? What have you done to intervene? Your expression of caring and friendship may be the one thing that saves them.

BE A FRIEND TO EVERYONE YOU MEET

Everyone who meets you should be better off because of it. Make that your goal. You may do it with a kind word, empathetic listening, or most powerfully, through your own example.

Decide right now to project positive energy to those around you. Be a force for good. Work on your own character traits in order to "shine with a brighter mirror." People will see your light. Spread it as far as you can.

Are you a positive force for others? Are they better off for having known you? What kind of an example do you set? Would people want to emulate you? Do you inspire others? Are you a valued friend?

REMEMBER, "NO MAN IS AN ISLAND"

The poet John Donne said, "Never ask for whom the bell tolls; it tolls for thee."[3] What did he mean? To understand, we must transport ourselves to England during that time, the sixteenth century. Back then, nearly everyone lived in rural farming villages. The church was the tallest building in town, and the church bell rang out for all important events. When it tolled, it announced to all the villagers out in their fields that a death had occurred. But rather than asking, "Who died?" John Donne wants us to realize that the death of any villager really means that a part of the village has died as well, since we're all connected in our humanity.

So it is on any team. We rely on each other. A victory for one is a victory for all. As Ben Franklin, one of the signers of the Declaration of Independence, said with gallows humor, "If we don't hang together, then they will surely hang us separately."[4]

As a leader, does your team hang together? Do they feel connected? Or do you treat them like interchangeable parts in a machine, overlooking their shared humanity?

"LOVE YOUR ENEMIES"

Throughout your life you will encounter people who, in spite of your best efforts, want no part of your friendship. No matter what you do, they resist your overtures of good will. Perhaps one day they'll come around; but realize too, that may never happen. However, don't let that change the way you are. Continue to treat them with kindness and respect. In other words, love them anyway. This is probably one of the most difficult things to do. Most of us find it impossible. But still, you should never give up on any human being. It may take years, but a breakthrough is always possible, and it's magical when it happens.

Whenever we have difficulty loving our enemies, we can look to our best role models for inspiration. Lincoln never allowed himself to be brought down to the level of those who hated him. Jesus Christ taught his followers with infinite patience and forbearance. And even when he was abandoned by his closest friends and turned over to his enemies for crucifixion, he had the courage to say, "Father, forgive them for they know not what they do."[5]

Loving our enemies is probably the toughest task we have in life. But it also has the potential to bear the most fruit.

BE READY TO THROW A LIFE RING

Naval vessels always have a lookout posted on the fantail, the stern of the ship. His most important job is to be alert for a man overboard, and throw him a life ring. The vigilance of that lookout means life or death for a man falling in the water. In most cases, it's his last chance to be saved.

There are times when we are like that lookout. We could literally be a friend's last chance for survival. He may be without hope, overcome by personal problems, addictions, or even contemplating suicide. If we're watchful, we'll recognize his call for help.

But recognizing it is only the first step. Now we must be willing to throw the life ring. This may be as simple as a kind or encouraging word, advising him to seek professional help, giving financial assistance, or just a willingness to listen. Never underestimate the impact you can have. It can make all the difference in the world to someone in need of rescue. It may even save his life.

Are you a good lookout? Are you overlooking signals that a friend is in trouble? What is your intuition telling you about a potential problem? More importantly, are you ready to throw a life ring?

FRIENDSHIP IS BASED ON RESPECT, NOT POPULARITY

Some people make the mistake of seeking popularity, thinking it will lead to friendship and respect. Usually they end up with neither.

It is better to stand up for your principles, not caring what people think. Trying to curry favor and be all things to all people will only frustrate you. People will see you as someone who leads by opinion polls—and not worthy of friendship or respect.

True friendships and inspiring leadership can be built only on a foundation of respect. Nothing else works.

Are you overly concerned with what people think? Are you swayed by public opinion, or steadfast? Is your leadership based on the bedrock of guiding principles, or do you change with shifting winds? Is popularity more important to you than respect? Do you make the mistake of thinking it will lead to true friendship?

NEVER UNDERESTIMATE THE POWER OF A KIND WORD

Everyone needs acknowledgment, to know they matter. An encouraging word has unbelievable power to motivate. But it must be absolutely sincere. Anything less undermines your credibility and does nothing for the person hearing it, except perhaps, to sow doubt in their own abilities, "Why am I receiving false praise?"

As a leader, open your eyes and manage by walking around. There's a lot of good happening around you. Your job is to notice it and acknowledge it! You'll never come close to seeing it all. But don't miss seeing as much as you can. That well-timed word of praise is energizing to your team and gives a remarkable boost to morale. They'll know you really care about them. And give acknowledgment as soon as you see it. It means far more than some award given long after the fact.

Are you aware of how much good is going on behind the scenes? Do you make an effort to acknowledge it? Are you stuck behind your desk? Do people on your team see you walking around every day, interested in them? Do you ask about their families in addition to their work? Or are all of your conversations with them merely superficial, lacking genuine interest? Are you missing a chance to be a true friend?

SEE THE GOOD IN PEOPLE

We often allow the faults of others to be magnified and overlook the good they really do. This can be especially true of our own family members or friends. We nag our children and spouses, or criticize friends and fellow workers to the point where we begin to believe they can't do anything right. Sadly, they also start believing this, and it becomes a self-fulfilling prophecy. They lose heart.

It's better to look for the good in others. Even when the negative actually does outweigh the positive, try to catch them in the act of doing something right, then build on it. Over time, you'll boost their self-esteem and they will seek to live up to the high opinion you have of them. Negative comments only tear them down.

Do you view people through a negative filter? How do you think that affects them? What steps can you take to view them in a different light? What are some positives you can see in their behavior that you can build on, right now?

Demonstrating through your actions that you're in their corner sends a powerful message. Most people will respond to that kind of positive reinforcement in a dramatic way. Be patient; you'll soon begin to see the effects.

YOU CAN'T DO IT ALONE

John Donne said it best, "No man is an island." While we may cling to the romanticized American folklore of the rugged individual, making it on his own, that's seldom the way it works in real life.

Sooner or later we realize that we can't do it all by ourselves. Henry Ford introduced the idea of the assembly line.[6] But it would remain a mere *idea* without workers to make it happen. Even athletes who play individual sports like golf and tennis have their coaches, nutritionists, and sports psychologists.

All of mankind's greatest achievements were team efforts. When we look more closely, even solo accomplishments most certainly had the early encouragement of parents, coaches, and family members. Only when we work together in concert do we reach our full potential as human beings.

We have written throughout this book about the reflections on leadership and certain values that were shared by our classmates from the Naval Academy. Without question, there is a bond of lifelong friendship that continues to resonate within this rather large "fraternity." Dave Poyer, classmate and noted author, writes that love and compassion are absolutely necessary to be a leader. The naval leaders portrayed in his novels clearly demonstrate a love for their sailors. They serve our nation and work together to make a difference. Members of this special seagoing fraternity are also aware that being on a strong and winning team means you can always depend on one another. It is a unique camaraderie that is difficult to express in mere words but is characterized by true love and friendship.

Are you a solo act? Are you so arrogant that you believe you did it without any assistance? If so, then you need to examine more closely all the ways people helped you along the way.

SPREAD THE LIGHT

All of us are on Earth for a purpose, each with certain talents. For some, that may be the ability to create magnificent works of art: the Statue of David, the Mona Lisa, and the Pieta. For others, it may be the ability to design and build architectural wonders: the Taj Mahal, Saint Peter's Basilica, the Great Pyramid, the Temple of Jerusalem. Still others may have the gift of music. Could anyone doubt for a moment that the amazing abilities of Mozart, Chopin, and Beethoven were gifts, something they were born with?

The ability to lead and motivate people is also a gift. Everyone has it to a certain degree. However, certain men and women throughout history have had this talent in abundance: Moses, Alexander the Great, Abraham Lincoln, Robert E. Lee, and Margaret Thatcher, to name a few. They stand out in their ability to lead and influence others.

We get into trouble, however, when we start thinking of ourselves as the source of any of these inborn talents. Like the lighthouses of old that guarded rocky shores, each had a brilliant source of light, a bright flame if you will. But that illuminating light is not our own. We can be only mirrors, reflecting that light to the far horizon. *We can polish the mirror, but we are never the flame.*

So what is our role in life? It is taking the gifts that have been given to us, polishing the mirror, and spreading the light as far as possible.

LOVE, THE MOST POWERFUL FORCE IN THE UNIVERSE

We spoke earlier of the Marines on Guadalcanal and the bond that existed between them. It is a friendship, which can be described only as love. That same bond has been demonstrated many times throughout history. In fact, mankind has risen to its greatest achievements when inspired by this most powerful force in the universe. Love is, without a doubt, the highest expression of our humanity.

The three hundred Spartans at Thermopylae were hopelessly outnumbered by thousands of invading Persians. Yet, led by their warrior king, Leonidas, they gladly died for each other, saving all of Greece.[7] Lord Nelson's men endured withering cannon fire at close range on the high seas because his leadership and the love they had for one another inspired them. Robert E. Lee's men worshiped him and willingly faced impossible odds for their beloved leader. Brave corpsmen in every historic battle have exposed themselves to lethal fire, without hesitation, to save wounded comrades.

The list of Medal of Honor winners numbers 3,459.[8] It echoes the theme of individual valor, love, and self-sacrifice. Yet even those stories are merely the tip of the iceberg when it comes to chronicling all of the acts of heroism that occurred in so many of America's conflicts. None of them would have even been possible if it hadn't been for the love fighting men and women felt for their comrades.

But love goes far beyond the battlefield. Who can discount the love that firefighters have for their fellow man as they risk their own lives on a daily basis? Or what love can match that which exists between parents and their children? All of these examples share one thing in common: placing others before self, the true definition of love.

Finally, we have the greatest example of love the world has ever known: a God who is the source of all love in the universe. He is the very same God who "so loved the world that He gave His only Son, so that everyone who believed in Him might not perish, but have eternal life."[9]

REFLECTION AND DISCUSSION

1. Do you think that we have forgotten the importance of friendship and love in our leadership today?

2. Do you agree with Mickey Mantle's observations about winning teams?

3. Discuss the effects of love and friendship—or lack of it—on some of your own teams, past and present.

4. Would you agree with the statement that mankind's greatest achievements have their source in love and friendship?

Chapter 16
Dignity, Decency, and Respect

"SO GOD CREATED HUMANKIND IN HIS IMAGE, IN THE IMAGE OF
GOD HE CREATED THEM: MALE AND FEMALE HE CREATED THEM."

GENESIS 1: 27

The University of Dayton's student handbook does an excellent job of capturing the essence of dignity, decency, and respect. While written specifically for the university, these principles are universal and apply to all of mankind:

> A primary assertion of both our religious and civil traditions is the inviolable dignity of each person. Recognition of and respect for the person are central to our life as Christians and are what allow us to pursue our common goals while being many diverse persons. Thus, discrimination, harassment, or any other conduct that diminishes the worth of a person is incompatible with our fundamental values as a decent, God-fearing nation.

Every person, regardless of race, color, creed, national origin, gender, age, or disability shall be treated with respect and dignity. No person shall be subject to any sexual, racial, psychological, physical, verbal or other similar harassment or abuse, or be denied equitable consideration for access to employment and the programs, services, and activities of the university.[1]

MADE IN HIS IMAGE

The Christian intellectual and moral tradition has always seen the human person as an image of God or a precious manifestation of God in our midst. All persons must be respected for their inherent dignity because they are the image of God. Often as humans we act in ways that are unfaithful to our dignity and to our call to be an image of God. Yet Christian moral and social teaching has always maintained that our first duty to a person is respect befitting a person made in the image of God.

The dignity of the human person has always been the starting point for Christianity's teaching against racism, ethnic hatred and violence, and harassment of others for any reason. Christianity is unambiguous in its expression of our obligation to not only respect the dignity of all people, but also to root out personal blindness and structural barriers that in any way keep people from realizing their dignity.

In their pastoral letter on racism in 1979, American bishops called attention to the fact that "Racism is a sin; a sin that divides the human family, blots out the image of God among specific members of that family and violates the fundamental human dignity of those called to be children of the same Father. Racism is not merely one sin among many, but it is a radical evil dividing the human family and denying the new creation of a redeemed world."[2]

THE "GOLDEN RULE," THE FOUNDATION FOR DIGNITY AND RESPECT

It's interesting that the most timeless principles cut across all ages, all religions, and all cultures. This is certainly true of the "Golden Rule." As Marcus Singer tells us, "The Golden Rule, in one version or another, has a prominent place in all major religions. The nearly universal acceptance of the Golden Rule by persons of considerable intelligence and divergent outlooks provides evidence that it is a fundamental ethical truth." Here are some of the ways it has been expressed:

Confucius: "We should behave to others as we wish others to behave to us."

Judaism: "What you dislike for yourself, do not do to anyone."

Hinduism: "Do nothing to thy neighbor which thou wouldst not have him do to thee thereafter."

Islam: "No one of you is a believer unless he loves for his brother what he loves for himself."

Buddhism: "Hurt not others with that which pains thyself."

Christianity: "Do unto others as you would have them do unto you."

No matter who we are, if we follow our personal interpretation of the Golden Rule, we will automatically treat others with dignity and respect.

SIX BASIC RULES HELP US UNDERSTAND RESPECT

The Josephson Institute of Ethics tells us that, in addition to the Golden Rule, there are six other rules to help us understand respect:

1. Honor the individual worth and dignity of others. People are not things. All of us have a basic right to be treated with dignity. Value and honor all people for themselves, not for what they can do for you or to you. No person should be used simply as the instrument of another's needs. Manipulating, mistreating, abusing, exploiting, or taking advantage of others is disrespectful. We would do well to remember the words of Immanuel Kant, "Every man is to be respected as an absolute end in himself; and it is a crime against the dignity that belongs to him as a human being to use him as a mere means for some external purpose."

2. Be courteous and civil. Using good manners and being civil are basic rules of respect. The simple ritual of saying "please," "thank you," and "excuse me" acknowledges the importance of others entitled to respect.

3. Honor reasonable social standards and customs. Judge others on their character, abilities, and conduct and not on such matters as race, religion, gender, where they live, how they dress, or the amount of money they have. Our behavior toward others should be based on accepted notions of taste, propriety, and decency. We honor traditions, customs, and beliefs important to others. To show and model respect, we honor reasonable social standards and customs including dressing, speaking, and acting in a manner that is neither offensive nor inappropriate in the context. For example, we do not utter profanities to teachers, make ethnic or racial slurs, or wear inappropriate clothing to a religious event.

4. Accept differences and judge on character and ability. People should be judged on their abilities and their character rather than their race, religion, gender, or political ideology. Intolerance, prejudice, and discrimination are disrespectful attitudes. Be tolerant, respectful, and accepting of those who are different from you. Listen to others and try to understand their points of view. We should remember the words of Jonathan Swift, "We have just enough religion to make us hate, but not enough to make us love one another."

5. Respect the autonomy of others. The duty of respect requires us to honor the inherent right of all people to autonomy. It is disrespectful to withhold information people need and want for making informed decisions about their own lives. All people, including maturing children, should have a say in decisions that affect them. We

show respect and teach responsibility by providing young people with the opportunity to participate in decisions that affect them.

6. Avoid actual or threatened violence. It is disrespectful to abuse, insult, demean, or physically harm any person. Resolve disagreements, respond to insults, and deal with anger peacefully and without violence. Even Elvis Presley showed himself to be a bit of a philosopher when he spoke this simple truth, "Animals don't hate, and we're supposed to be better than they are."[3]

WHAT IT MEANS FOR LEADERS

Dave Howe, a graduate of the Class of 1971, served over twenty years on active duty and in the reserves as a surface warfare officer. He climbed the ladder of success in business in his home state of Texas and joined Enron as it surged to the top of the market as a company shining with success. As a VP at Enron, he witnessed first hand the results of poor leadership and financial greed. Moreover, there was little respect given to shareholders and employees when the collapse became inevitable. With little or no notice, he was let go and is currently the Vice President of Institutional Trust Services at JP Morgan Chase. One of his most cherished values in a leader is respect. He knows that to be an effective leader, you must care for the people who work for you, which includes consistent recognition of their contributions.

Another '71 graduate ran his own business for a number of years before accepting the challenges as a leader at a different successful company. But he became disappointed and frustrated when the newly appointed president of the company treated him with disrespect, especially after his many years of faithful service.

He saw the writing on the wall when it became apparent that the new president had no desire to work with him or his people. Sadly, the new boss was totally ignorant of the leadership and manpower required to run a successful sales team. To make matters worse, he was told he had to layoff many valued and dedicated employees who were critical to the sales force. Of course, this had a tremendous negative impact on the company, but more importantly, on the lives of the employees and their families. In good conscience, he had no other recourse but to resign over the total lack of effective communication and good leadership.

Without an atmosphere of mutual respect, failure is almost always the result. This truth applies whether we're talking about two people, a family, corporations, or nations. It is a leader's key responsibility to create an environment that fosters respect. Leaders who fail to appreciate how important this is may cause a fundamental breakdown of morale within their organizations. Courtesy and respect for others must be carefully integrated into every segment of the workplace, the family, and society.

BROWN VERSUS THE BOARD OF EDUCATION

Our own history has many lessons to teach us about dignity, decency, and respect. Sadly, much of that involves learning from our mistakes, our failure to live up to the ideals upon which this country was founded. As Lincoln reminded the nation in his famous address at Gettysburg, we had lived with the egregious evil of slavery for "four score and seven years." Lincoln himself, in his succinct and eloquent fashion, put it this way, "As I would not be a slave, so I would not be a master. This expresses my idea of democracy. What differs from this, to the extent of the difference, is no democracy."[4]

After the Civil War, that evil was abolished, but the diseases of prejudice and discrimination lived on in a far more virulent form. Beginning with Reconstruction, we continued to delude ourselves with the notion that "separate but equal" fulfilled the promises in our Declaration of Independence and our Constitution. In fact, with the Supreme Court decision of *Plessy v. Ferguson*, it became the law of the land. It wasn't until the landmark case, *Brown v. the Board of Education*, decided sixty years later in 1954, that "separate but equal" was exposed for the gross injustice it was.

That marked the beginning of one of the most turbulent decades in our history, when courageous heroes like Martin Luther King, Rosa Parks, Medgar Evers, and so many others literally put their lives on the line in the battle for racial equality. They paid a high price, often the ultimate price, but they advanced the causes of racial justice, dignity, decency, and respect farther than they had ever gone before.

The battle is certainly not won, but we've come a long way in fulfilling the original promise of our Founding Fathers. As former

Chairman of the Joint Chiefs of Staff, Colin Powell, was the top-ranking man in uniform for the entire armed forces. He also became the first African American Secretary of State. Dr. Condoleeza Rice serves as the President's most trusted National Security Adviser. Black coaches and athletes are well established, even in the Deep South. Oprah Winfrey has her own syndicated television show and reaches millions. Michael Jordan is one of the most influential figures in American advertising. Children of every background want "to be like Mike." Our most prestigious universities have opened their doors to all races, creeds, and colors. It's no time to rest on our laurels, but we can certainly look back with a measure of pride at how far we've come. And we can use this retrospective look to encourage our efforts in the journey ahead. We haven't arrived yet, but we're getting there.[5]

CONCLUDING THOUGHTS

Dignity, decency, and respect are spiritual in origin. They ultimately flow from a source deep within the leader's soul. They shine most brightly through the leader's own example. To the degree that he treats his people with dignity, decency, and respect, so too will his followers spread that light throughout the rest of the team, in effect, mirroring their leader's behavior.

But isn't this always the way the great leaders of history have influenced their followers? Lincoln's dignity, decency, and humanity could be sensed by all who knew him. It was the secret of what we might call today "his charisma." He was a brilliant, yet humble man. He would often say, "The Lord must love the common man; that's why he made so many of us." His decency and innate common sense got us through the most dangerous period in our country's history, where arguably, the fate of the nation hung in the balance.

UCLA Coach John Wooden was the same way. Like Lincoln, he began life on a humble farm where he learned old-fashioned values of dignity, decency, and respect from his father, Joshua Hugh Wooden. He carried these ideals deep within his character as a three-time all-American at Purdue, and later at UCLA, as the only coach in collegiate history to win ten national championships. During one stretch, UCLA won seven titles in a row.

John Wooden, arguably the most renowned coach in college basketball history, had these insights on respect:

"The most essential thing for a leader to have is the respect of those under his or her supervision. It starts with giving them respect.

"You must make it clear that you are working together. Those under your supervision are not working for you but with you, and you all have a common goal.

"Remember, you can have respect for a person without necessarily liking that individual. Coach Amos Alonzo Stagg said, 'I loved all my players. I didn't like them all, but I did love them all.' What does that mean?

"You love your children, but you may not like some of the things they do. We are instructed, 'Love thy neighbor as thyself.' That doesn't mean we have to like everything our neighbor does. That has nothing to do with our love for them.

"You must have respect, which is a part of love, for those under your supervision. Then they will do what you ask and more. They'll go the extra distance, make the extra effort in trying to accomplish the most they can within the framework of the team.

"If they don't respect their leader, people just punch the clock in and out. There is no clock-watching when a leader has respect."[6]

Coach Wooden treated every one of his players with deep respect. Whether they were the star player, or the fifteenth man on the bench, they were important to the coach, and he made sure they knew it. He likened his greatest players, like Kareem Abdul-Jabbar and Bill Walton, to "powerful engines." But he was quick to point out that the "lug nuts" were just as important to the success of the team. If they fell off, this finely tuned racecar would go off the track. He remembers his team managers just as fondly as the stars and made sure they knew their contributions were no less significant to the overall success of the team. Coach Wooden would not allow discrimination of any kind. A writer once asked one of his star black players, Curtis Rowe, "What kind of racial problems do you have on the UCLA team?" He replied, "Coach doesn't see color."

Custodians of visitors' locker rooms remarked that UCLA players always left the locker room as neat as they found it, and better than any other visiting team. The reason? Coach Wooden insisted that his players show respect for the hospitality they had been given. It was part of his nature and upbringing; it became part of theirs.[7]

Leaders like Lincoln, Wooden, Lombardi, Rockne, Leahy, Gandhi, Lee, and Mother Teresa had no problem keeping their egos in check because they had no egos to get in the way in the first place. They used example as their most powerful leadership tool. Their own dignity, decency, and humanity shine as beacons for those who follow them.

REFLECTION AND DISCUSSION

1. "Racism is not merely one sin among many, but it is a radical evil dividing the human family and denying the new creation of a redeemed world." Do you agree or disagree with this statement?

2. Coach Amos Alonzo Stagg said, "I loved all my players. I didn't like them all, but I did love them all." What does that mean?

3. Would you agree or disagree that the Golden Rule is the foundation for dignity and respect?

4. Some historians say that the abolition of slavery was only a first step. *Brown* v. *Board of Education* was the next great leap in the pursuit of racial justice in America. Do you agree or disagree?

5. Who were your own role models for dignity, decency, and respect? Explain why.

Chapter 17
Faith, Spirit, and Spiritual Roots

"In God We Trust."

U.S. Coins and Currency

Spirit deals with the intangible elements of leadership. We are not just referring to a religious viewpoint but those things that civilizations throughout the ages have always valued such as honor, courage, commitment, truth, loyalty, friendship, family, goodness, respect, and an acknowledgment of a Higher Power.

Our Founding Fathers were deeply aware of these intangibles. They embedded them in our Declaration of Independence and our Constitution ("...endowed by their Creator with certain, inalienable rights, among them life, liberty, and the pursuit of happiness."). We print "In God We Trust" on our money and open each session of Congress with a prayer. A chaplain presides at many military and government ceremonies and our President is sworn in with his hand on the Bible.

To ignore the power of spirit in our leadership is to miss the essence of who we are as leaders, and who we are as a nation. Sometimes we avoid talk of spirituality because it's considered the soft side of leadership, too touchy-feely. But in truth, working with people is all "soft stuff."

Perhaps we deny this dimension in ourselves out of embarrassment, because it's too private, or because we want to be politically correct. But it's a mistake to ignore our spiritual roots. We must connect with our souls and things of the spirit in order to have any chance of inspiring those we lead.

Most of the Founding Fathers were God-fearing, Christian men. While they were totally against a state-mandated religion, they certainly had no intention of removing all things of the spirit from this new experiment called the United States of America. They knew that spirit was already deeply embedded in the American culture. It made the American Revolution a worthy cause and was the essence of Lincoln's leadership during the dark days of the Civil War when the fate of our young nation hung in the balance. In fact, if Lincoln hadn't captured the true reason for the war, slavery, Great Britain might have become an ally of the South, resulting in a far different outcome. But Lincoln showed that the North's desire to abolish slavery was a noble cause worth fighting for, and Great Britain agreed. Having already abolished slavery themselves, the British could not support the southern cause.

Ronald Reagan, our fortieth President, was a man who respected people and institutions, trusting in the innate power of the individual to do the right thing. Nevertheless, his worldview and early spiritual foundation shaped his life and even his political beliefs. When he was a child in the early 1920s, schools taught the truth about how our nation began and about the principles of faith America was founded upon. There was never a contradiction between Ronald Reagan's inner life of faith and his view of America's heritage as "one nation under God." [1]

During the Presidential debates in 1980, he made the following claim, "Going around this country, I have found a greater hunger in America for a spiritual revival; for a belief that law must be based on a higher law; for a return to values and traditions we once had. Our government, in its most sacred documents—the Constitution and the Declaration of Independence—speaks of man being created, of a Creator; that we are indeed one nation under God."[2]

Reagan, more than one hundred years after Lincoln, faced a different war from that of his predecessor. But like the sixteenth President, Reagan stayed in deep spiritual prayer during the Cold War for guidance from above as he constantly sought divine counsel for peace and understanding.[3]

Throughout their lives, Lincoln and Reagan often defined their leadership in spiritual terms. That made both of them two of our most powerful leaders. Spirit is as much of a part of leadership today as it was then. It is the essence of leadership. Without spirit, good leadership is impossible.

LET YOUR SPIRIT SHINE

It is said that Mother Teresa lit up a room by her mere presence. Her spirit touched everyone around her.

We've all felt the powerful influence of charismatic people. It's something we experience at an intangible level, not easily defined, but real nonetheless. Abraham Lincoln, Robert E. Lee, Martin Luther King, and Gandhi all had this undeniable power. What is it about them that projected such an aura?

Simply, it is a lifetime of selfless sacrifice and devotion to others that builds a spirit of such immense power. Throughout their lives, they remained true to their guiding principles. This enabled them to lift up and inspire everyone they met. Their characters, polished through years of service to others, shine like beacons even today, long after their deaths.

Does your spirit illuminate the surrounding darkness like a beacon? Are you building a character that will influence others for years to come? Will you leave a legacy?

"TO THINE OWN SELF BE TRUE..."

Shakespeare told us, "To thine own self be true, and it follows as the night the day, that thou cannot then be false to any man."

Many of our problems begin with kidding ourselves. We pretend we are something we're not, make phony excuses to ourselves, or rationalize our own behavior. It all boils down to pride and ego. We are reluctant to look at our true selves, because deep down inside, we know we are lacking in many qualities we wish we had. And we certainly don't want others to discover our secret.

But that brutally honest self-appraisal is just what we need for true growth. It's a starting point. It will allow us to become the individuals we would really like to be. When we are honest with ourselves, we no longer have to play games with other people. We cast off the burden of trying to be someone we're not. We can then begin the lifelong task of daily self-improvement.

Do you know who you really are? Do you have the courage to make an honest self-appraisal, in spite of what you may discover? Do you realize that, while painful, this can be very liberating and lead to great personal growth?

RECOGNIZE A HIGHER POWER

If you think you can manage to get through life on your own without any help, you're sadly mistaken. Whether you're a Zen Buddhist, American Indian who worships The Great Spirit, Taoist, Moslem, Hindu, Jew, or Christian, most people somehow realize that there is a Higher Power at work among us. All cultures throughout history have been drawn to their own concept of a Supreme Being. It's an awareness hardwired into our human nature. It's a common bond we all share.

We may pretend that God doesn't exist, but the evidence to the contrary is overwhelming. One look at Nature tells us the world is not some random event. All of this order and design is, without a doubt, the work of a Grand Architect. To deny his existence would be like saying you could take all the parts of a Chevy, put them in a large box, give them an infinite amount of shaking, and eventually see a fully assembled automobile. It will never happen!

Despite the denial of a minority of atheists and agnostics, it should comfort us that God, however we choose to know Him, does indeed exist. He is there to help us. All we have to do is ask. While He doesn't necessarily answer our prayers in the way we expect, He does answer them all, in His own way and in His own time.

Don Jenkins from the Class of 1971 has been in corporate America since leaving the Navy as a young officer. Since his number-one role model is Jesus Christ, he has always been drawn to Godly men. He sees Jesus as the original servant leader who invested in people one-on-one. To see Jesus in others has been the delight of Don's professional life and has helped make him the compassionate leader he is today.

As a leader, do you acknowledge a Higher Power? Do you allow Him to guide you? Without a deep and abiding faith in the Almighty, you've lost your most powerful resource.

DON'T SEEK EARTHLY REWARDS

Sad and empty is the man who spends his whole life accumulating material wealth. In Charles Dickens's *A Christmas Carol*, Ebenezer Scrooge sees his possible fate: His possessions become links in a heavy chain, which he fashions around his own neck, to be hauled around for all eternity, just like his former partner, Jacob Marley.

Did you ever notice how the "rich and famous" are often the most unhappy and least fulfilled? Each extravagant purchase they make gives only temporary pleasure. Soon they are seeking something bigger and better—bigger car, bigger boat, bigger house, and bigger airplane. But that only perpetuates the cycle, leaving them frustrated once again. Contrast them to Mother Teresa, who spent a lifetime of service to the poorest of the poor. She lacked earthly possessions, but radiated joy and happiness.

In the end, we will be judged by the size of our hearts, not the size of our bank accounts. Whoever said "you can't take it with you" and "the best things in life are free" was absolutely right.

Are you fashioning your own chain of earthly possessions like Ebenezer Scrooge? Do you equate money with success? Do you judge people by the cars they drive, where they live, or their titles? Do you think you can ever buy true happiness?

FOLLOW THE "GOLDEN RULE"

There's a good reason they call it the "Golden Rule." If everyone followed that one premise, "Do unto others as you would have them do unto you," the world would be a better place for us all.

It's so simple. And yet how many times do we catch ourselves not following it? We end up looking out for our own happiness, and ourselves as if we were alone in the world. We often fail to recognize the impact we have on others. But as John Donne tells us, "No man is an island." What we do affects other people. In the long run, what hurts others will also hurt us; what helps others will help us.

Do you follow the Golden Rule? Is it a part of your life's philosophy? Is it a norm for your team?

DON'T EXPECT THE SCALES TO BALANCE

There is one simple truth that we have to come to grips with: Life isn't fair. If we expect the scales to balance, we're only going to be disappointed. Bad things *do* happen to good people.

So what should we do about it? Simply, do what is right and things will usually work out for the best. Sure, you'll have setbacks and encounter people who don't play by the rules. But you'll sleep well at night with a clear conscience.

Rest assured, in the final judgment at the end of our lives, the Ultimate Judge will weigh what we've done and the scales *will* balance. "Blessed are they who hunger and thirst for justice, for they shall have their fill."[4]

Do you waste precious time and energy complaining that life isn't fair? Look around. There are many people in this world who have been dealt a tougher hand than you have. Every day, they cope with far more misery, hardship, and injustice than you ever will. Remember the old saying, "I once complained that I had no shoes, but then I met a man who had no feet."

"EVIL TRIUMPHS WHEN GOOD MEN DO NOTHING"

Neville Chamberlain signed the Munich Pact in September 1938, negotiating with Hitler to settle the question of Czechoslovakia. The agreement signed by Britain, France, Italy, and Germany gave the Sudetenland, a resource rich area of Czechoslovakia (one-fifth of the country on the German speaking border) to Germany with other areas going to Hungary and Poland.

Returning in triumph to Britain at Heston Airport on September 30, Chamberlain told a cheering crowd, "I believe it is peace in our time."[5]

The peace did not last long. Germany took the rest of Czechoslovakia six months after the agreement was signed. Less than a year later, the world was once again at war. Appeasement in the face of evil never works. It merely promotes greater evil.

Do you have the courage to confront evil? Or does your passive attitude allow it to flourish? Do you remain silent to avoid making waves? As a leader, do people know what principles you stand for?

DON'T LET EVIL DISCOURAGE YOU

It's hard not to become discouraged when we open the paper every morning and read about the evil all around us. Rapes, bombings, genocide, child molestation, sniper attacks, murders, and mayhem fill the pages. All of us have had the thought, "What is this world coming to!"

But perhaps we can take comfort in this fact: The reason it's news is that it's *the exception*. The vast majority of people in the world are good, and every day they are making positive contributions in their own little corners of the world. In fact, their basic goodness is so commonplace it isn't newsworthy.

So don't let evil discourage you. Spread your own light every day and resolve to make the world a better place. The collective contributions of the good people in this world far outweigh the bad.

Have you allowed yourself to be overwhelmed, disheartened, and immobilized by the evil around you? Have you overlooked the good that actually exists and your own ability to contribute to a better world? Realize that good is destined to one day triumph over evil, and you have a large part to play in that ultimate victory. Let that empower your leadership in a troubled world.

"DON'T TAKE IT PERSONALLY"

There's no question that words can be damaging and hurtful—if we let them! But in the book *The Four Agreements* we are reminded, "Don't take it personally."

Often, the harmful things people say reveal far more about themselves than they do about us. They are usually projecting their own shortcomings or feelings of inadequacy.

The best response to criticism is to be brutally honest with yourself. Evaluate it for elements of truth. Are several people saying the same thing? Is there a consistent theme? If so, work on a plan for self-improvement. Use their comments to become a better person.

But unfair or unjust criticism is entirely different. Never allow it to damage your self-esteem. It really tells you more about the critic than it does yourself.

Do you evaluate criticism honestly for potential self-improvement? Are you able to ignore unjust criticism? Are you careful with your own words? Do you guard against backbiting on your team? Do you air differences on your team in a constructive way?

MAKE A DIFFERENCE

People often ask, "What difference can just one person make? What's the use of even trying?" But John F. Kennedy won the 1960 presidential election by an average of one vote per precinct across the nation. President Andrew Johnson, Lincoln's successor, was impeached, but stayed in office because of one vote.[6]

Loren Eiseley, in his book of essays, *The Star Throwers*, tells an interesting story: A young man on the beach observes an older man stooping down, picking something up, and throwing it as far as he could back into the ocean. He did this over and over. As the young man got closer, he could see that the older man was picking up starfish.

He asked him, "Hey, there are thousands of starfish along this beach, as far as the eye can see. Just what are you doing?" "Well," the man replied, "these starfish were left stranded at high tide, and I'm saving them by throwing them back in the ocean." "Are you crazy?" the young man asked. "You'll never make a difference with the thousands out here." The older man just ignored the question, reached down, and flung another one into the sea saying, "Made a difference to that one, didn't I?"[7]

Where would we be without Abraham Lincoln, George Washington, Rosa Parks, Martin Luther King, Jr., and hundreds more? Do you still doubt that one person can make a difference?

UNDERSTAND THE POWER OF FORGIVENESS

We often look at forgiveness—which, in itself, is hard enough—as something we do for other people.

But if you examine it more closely, forgiveness is also something we do for ourselves. Remembering slights, holding grudges, and seeking revenge is like acid, eating away its container. If we hold anger inside, it damages us. And the longer we hold on to it, the more damage it does, physically, mentally, and spiritually.

Forgiveness is liberating, both asking for it and granting it. When we ask others to forgive us, it allows us to let go of the guilt for past transgressions. This holds true, whether they choose to forgive us or not. When we forgive others, it doesn't mean that we've forgotten what they did, just that we're not going to let it poison us anymore.

The Lord's Prayer says, "Forgive us our trespasses, as we forgive those who trespass against us." A frightening double-edged sword, isn't it? It asks us to examine our own ability to forgive others, because that's the standard that will be applied to us. George Herbert tells us, "He who cannot forgive breaks the bridge over which he himself must cross."

How well are you able to ask for and grant forgiveness? Are you aware that holding grudges and harboring thoughts of revenge damages your spirit? Viewed in that light, does hurting yourself even make sense?

UNWIND AND RECHARGE YOUR BATTERIES

Life is not a continuous sprint. Even NASCAR drivers know that they can't keep the pedal to the metal, red-lining the engine for the entire race. They must pace themselves and their finely tuned machines in order to finish without breaking down.

Yet, we often insist on burning ourselves out, failing to take a needed break and unwind. In the long run, we do great physical, mental, and spiritual damage to ourselves. We not only risk being unable to complete the immediate task at hand, but more importantly, our life's work.

Easing off on the accelerator is an absolute necessity. Take a break and do something relaxing and enjoyable, even if it seems a frivolous waste of time. In actuality, it's an investment in your own physical, mental, and emotional health. You'll quickly discover renewed energy. Your creativity will be released and your spirit will soar. In the long run, you'll accomplish far more than if you kept your nose to the grindstone without taking a break.

Do you allow time to recharge your batteries, or are you continually burning the candle at both ends? Would your team call you a slave driver? When was the last time you got away from the office together and just had some fun? When was the last company picnic? Were families invited? Do your people look tired? Are they leaving work in time to have dinner at home? What kind of hours are they keeping? Do you even know? Do you promote a physical fitness program? Or are the only benefits you offer to your employees monetary?

SEEK BALANCE IN YOUR LIFE

Remember that you are body, mind, and spirit. All of these must be nourished. Neglect any one area, and the others suffer.

The bodily dimension is easy to understand. Eat the right foods and get enough rest and exercise. Challenge yourself physically, but don't overdo it. If you get injured, allow enough time to heal.

We also need mental stimulation. This may come through reading, doing crossword puzzles and brainteasers, writing our thoughts in a journal, watching educational TV (while making sure to avoid the mindless drivel that too often passes for entertainment).

Taking care of the spirit is not as easily defined. It involves such things as humor and laughter, the enjoyment of music and art, meditation, watching a sunset, listening to waves breaking on a secluded beach, religious worship, service to others, being with friends and family. Often a favorite physical activity can have a spiritual dimension as well: snow skiing through deep powder, surfing the perfect wave, or kayaking down a scenic river.

Unless we recognize and nourish all three dimensions, we will be out of balance and incomplete as human beings.

Do you take care of your body, mind, and spirit? Are you overlooking any of these dimensions? Do you make time on your schedule for regular exercise, family and friends, quiet reflection, reading, and recreation? Do you realize that they are just as important to your well being and success? Or do you focus only on your job at work, to the exclusion of everything else?

TAKE A STAND—CHARACTER AND ETHICS MATTER

You're either a spectator in life, or a player. You either live by your principles, or abandon them. There is no middle ground.

As we said before, "Evil triumphs when good men do nothing." Pity the man or woman who has nothing they're willing to die for. Is that even a life worth living?

How about you, do you stand up for what you believe in, or easily surrender to adversity? In your own life, do character and ethics matter?

We've touched on the lives of many of our classmates from the Class of '71. From humble beginnings, they came to know one of the most important truths life has to teach us: Character is the foundation of leadership. Without question, character and ethics do matter. In an ambiguous world, inspiring leaders stand tall and make ethical decisions that provide moral clarity for the people they lead. A leader must understand that people will follow him only if they know what he stands for—and equally important, what he won't stand for. Character and ethics *do* matter.

REFLECTION AND DISCUSSION

1. As a nation, do you think we have strayed from our spiritual roots?

2. Would you agree that human beings are body, mind, and spirit and that all of these dimensions are important to leadership development?

3. Do you believe that "evil triumphs when good men do nothing"?

4. How do you respond to criticism? Is it the way you should respond?

5. Give your own examples of how one person "made a difference."

Epilogue

We wrote this book because we are convinced that in a society burdened with political correctness and ever-shifting values, character and ethics do matter. People truly want inspirational leaders who have depth of character. We repeat our initial premise: Without strong character and integrity, inspirational leadership is impossible.

We strongly believe that ethical behavior is defined by our character and has a deep connection with our spiritual roots. At the center of this reality are family, friends, and faith.

We have used some of history's great leaders and our own Naval Academy classmates and friends throughout this book as examples. We realize that everyone reading this book will have his own personal favorites, different from ours. But what is most important is that we use these great men and women, whomever we may choose, as beacons of light in our own journey to become better leaders.

As of this writing, the world closely watches the United States in its quest to overcome the threat of world terror and establish peace and justice for all freedom loving people. Our military men and women continue to fight for this noble cause. We have dedicated this book to all of them and are proud that classmates from the Class of '71 are still leading our troops and our nation to the ultimate victory over terror.

In 2003, the Navy football team won the Commander-in-Chief Trophy, representing the best service academy football team. Presenting their award in April 2004 in the East Room of the White House, President George W. Bush said, "One of the things that the young men and women at the Naval Academy learn is leadership, how important it is to be a leader, what it means to lead, how one sets standards and brings people to a higher calling. We expect officers who wear the uniform to have character and to cherish the view that failure is not an option. Winning is vital if you're a football player or an officer in the Navy or Marine Corps. It takes hard work, and I don't know a lot of people who work hard so they can go out and lose. But I do know that what is taking place now is that you are preparing to lead our nation in a time of war and I am confident that you will follow your predecessors serving overseas and perform brilliantly. We have a mission in this nation, and that is not only to make ourselves secure from an enemy which hates our freedom, but at the same time, spread freedom so that the world will be more peaceful, so people have a chance to live with dignity and hope. And members of the classes before you from the Naval Academy understand that mission, and they're accomplishing it with great class and dignity."

We have dedicated this book to the young men and women who continue to serve our great country as true patriots in order to protect us from all enemies, both foreign and domestic. The United States Naval Academy Class of 1971 has dedicated a special Battle Memorial Arch at the Navy-Marine Corps Memorial Stadium in Annapolis, Maryland. The inscription on the dedication plaque reads:

We honor here our classmates and all who served their country during Operation Enduring Freedom—our Nation's earliest response to the terrorist attacks against the United States of America on September 11, 2001. These classmates and patriotic Americans embraced the concept that we inherited freedom from our ancestors—a precious freedom we must continue to defend as long as terrorists threaten our democratic principles, our homeland, and our American way of life. But our task is to do more than just honor those who have contributed. As President Lincoln said in his Gettysburg address: "It is for us the living, rather, to be dedicated to the unfinished work, which they who fought here have thus far so nobly advanced."

U.S. Naval Academy, Class of 1971

Endnotes

Introduction

1. James Calvert. 1971. *The Naval Profession.* New York: McGraw-Hill.
2. *The United States Naval Academy 2000-2001 Catalog.* 2000. Annapolis, MD: U.S. Naval Academy.

Chapter 1

1. A Nation at Risk. 1994. *USA Research*, 2nd Edition.

Chapter 2

1. *The Random House College Dictionary*, Revised Edition, 1980.
2. Ibid.
3. Karl Montor. 1987. *Naval Leadership: Voices of Experience.* Naval Institute Press.
4. Cal Thomas. 2001. *The Wit and Wisdom of Cal Thomas.* Promise Press.

Chapter 3

1. *Eleventh Annual Conference of Superintendents of the Academies of the Armed Forces Record of Proceedings.* April 1969. Annapolis, MD: U.S. Naval Academy.
2. James M. Kouzes and Barry Z. Posner. 1995. *The Leadership Challenge.* Jossey-Bass.

Chapter 4

1. James Webb. 1985. *A Sense of Honor.* Naval Institute Press.
2. C.S. Lewis. 2001. *Mere Christianity.* Harper Press.

3. Robert A. Filton. 1997. *Leadership: Quotations from the World's Greatest Motivators.* Westview Press.
4. Ken Burns. PBS documentary, *The Civil War.*
5. Frank J. Wilson. April 1947. "Character and Destiny." *Colliers.*
6. Colonel Bob Cabana, USMC, was designated by NASA to be the Ombudsman in the aftermath of the 2003 *Columbia* Space Shuttle disaster.

Chapter 5

1. Reid F. Buckley. 2002. *USA Today: The Stunning Incoherence of American Civilization.* Pen Press.
2. Captain Frank Culbertson, USN (Ret.), commanding the International Space Station, was in orbit above the Earth on September 11, 2001. His reflections are based on his eyewitness account while passing over New York City and Washington, D.C. within hours of the early morning attack by terrorists on our nation. Ironically, he was not only a classmate of Chic Burlingame but also was his good friend and fellow member of the popular Naval Academy Drum and Bugle Corps in 1968 and 1969.
3. Personal letters released by NASA and Captain Frank Culbertson, USN (Ret.), in September and October 2001. These letters were sent by Captain Frank Culbertson, USNA '71, to his family, friends, and classmates from Annapolis, and were his reflections of the tragedy as seen from space while he commanded the International Space Station.
4. VADM Tim Keating has been selected for his 4th star and will assume command as Commander-in-Chief of the Northern Command and NORAD in November 2004; LTGen John Sattler assumed command of the 1st Marine Expeditionary Force in August 2004.
5. The Naval Academy Class of 1971 has dedicated a Memorial Battle Arch at the Navy-Marine Corps Memorial Stadium in Annapolis, Maryland, named "Enduring Freedom" in honor of those men and women who continue to serve their country in the War on Terror.
6. William J. Bennett. 2002. *Why We Fight.* Regnery Publishing, Inc.

Chapter 7

1. William Novak. 1984. *Iacocca : An Autobiography.*
2. Stephen Covey. 1989. *The Seven Habits of Highly Effective People.*
3. David B. Givens. 2003. *Worldbook Online Reference Center.*
4. Mark Twain. 1897. *Following the Equator.* Hartford, CT: American Publishing Co.

5.   David B. Givens. 2003. *Worldbook Online Reference Center.*
6.   Ibid.
7.   Ken Burns. 1990. PBS documentary, *The Civil War,*
8.   Ibid.
9.   David B. Givens. 2003. *Worldbook Online Reference Center.*
10. Naval Historical Center website.
11. "NOAA Earth Science Missions Anomaly Report," GSFC/POES Project/480/ K. Halterman, September 6, 2003, Lockheed Martin, Sunnyvale, CA.

Chapter 8

1.   100th Battalion of the 442 Infantry Regiment (Nisei soldiers) ("homeofheroes.com" website).
2.   Matthew 18:6.
3.   Haddon Klingberg. 2001. *When Life Calls Out to Us: The Love and Lifework of Viktor and Elly Frankl.*

Chapter 9

1.   Stephen Covey. 1989. *The Seven Habits of Highly Effective People.*
2.   Johann Christoph Arnold. 2003. *Seeking Peace, Notes and Conversations Along the Way.*
3.   Ibid.
4.   Ibid.
5.   Branch Rickey was the General Manager of the Brooklyn Dodgers when he signed Jackie Robinson, breaking the color barrier in major league baseball.
6.   Haddon Klingberg. 2001. *When Life Calls Out to Us : The Love and Lifework of Viktor and Elly Frankl.*
7.   Executive Order 9981, Harry Truman, July 26, 1948, establishing the President's Committee on Equality of Treatment and Opportunity in the Armed Forces.
8.   Carroll Kilpatrick. Sunday, October 21, 1973. "Nixon Forces Firing of Cox; Richardson, Ruckelshaus Quit President Abolishes Prosecutor's Office; FBI Seals Records." *Washington Post.*
9.   Chester G. Hearn. 2002. *Tracks in the Sea: Matthew Fontaine Maury and the Mapping of the Oceans.*
10. John Lienhard. 1988. "The Engines of Our Ingenuity, Number 1432: Decisiveness." University of Houston.

Chapter 10

1. William Shakespeare. *Hamlet.*
2. Phil Jackson. 1996. *Sacred Hoops, Spiritual Lessons of a Hardwood Warrior.*
3. John Wooden. 1988. *They Call Me Coach.*
4. Mark 10: 35–45.
5. Carroll Kilpatrick. Sunday, November 18, 1973. "Nixon Tells Editors, 'I'm Not a Crook.'" *Washington Post.*
6. Leona Helmsley quoted in *The New York Times*, July 12, 1989. "We don't pay taxes. Only the little people pay taxes."
7. Lord Acton. 1887. In a letter to Bishop Mandell Creighton.
8. Captain R. Stewart Fisher, USN (Ret.) reflects on his days as a Naval Aviator in helicopter squadrons.
9. Ibid.

Chapter 11

1. October 29, 1941, U.K., Prime Minister Winston Churchill speech at Harrow School.
2. William Novak. 1984. *Iacocca: An Autobiography.*
3. "The Journey of 1000 Miles…." Ancient Chinese proverb.
4. Luke 23: 34.
5. Rick Reilly. Oct. 20, 2003. "Worth the Wait." *Sports Illustrated.*
6. "I Have a Dream," speech by Dr. Martin Luther King at the Lincoln Memorial, August 28, 1963.
7. George E. Koskimaki. 2002. *D-Day With The Screaming Eagles.*

Chapter 12

1. Matthew 20:16.
2. John 13: 8-9.
3. *Sea of Glory: A Novel Based on the True WWII Story of the Four Chaplains and the U.S.A.T. Dorchester*, Ken Wales and David Poling.
4. John F. Kennedy's inaugural address, Washington, D.C. January 20, 1961.
5. The History Channel.
6. *Democracy in America*, published in two parts (the first in 1835, the second in 1840), the great work of Alexis de Tocqueville.
7. Hank Nuwer. 1998. *The Legend of Jesse Owens.*
8. Ibid.
9. "Catholic Information Center" website.
10. Ibid.

11. "Jimmy Carter and Habitat," Habitat for Humanity website.
12. Haddon Klingberg. 2001. *When Life Calls Out to Us: The Love and Life work of Viktor and Elly Frankl.*

Chapter 13

1. "Live with Dennis Miller," his HBO television series.
2. Proverbs 16: 18.
3. Genesis 3: 19.
4. Jone Johnson Lewis. 2003. *Wisdom Quotes: Quotations to Inspire and Challenge.*
5. "The Wizard of Menlo Park," Digital History website.
6. "The Rise and Fall of the Spartans." The History Channel.
7. John Reuben Thompson, 2001. *Lee to the Rear.*
8. Jon T. Hoffman. 2001. *Chesty: The Story of Lieutenant General Lewis B. Puller, USMC.*

Chapter 14

1. Remarks by Gen. Charles C. Krulak to the Naval Academy Leadership Conference, 5 January 1996.
2. Ed Ruggero. 2004. *Academy Leadership.*
3. Remarks by Gen. Charles C. Krulak to the Naval Academy Leadership Conference, 5 January 1996.
4. Dennis Perkins. 2000. *Leading at the Edge: Leadership Lessons from the Extraordinary Saga of Shackleton's Antarctic Expedition.*
5. Matthew 11: 29.
6. Matthew 19: 14.
7. Matthew 18: 16.
8. Luke 5: 31.
9. John 11: 35.
10. Matthew 23: 23.
11. Matthew 11: 28.
12. John 15: 13.

Chapter 15

1. William Manchester. 2002. *Goodbye, Darkness: A Memoir of the Pacific War.*
2. Mickey Mantle. 1989. *Mickey Mantle: The American Dream Comes to Life.*
3. John Donne. 1620. Meditation XVII: "No Man Is An Island."

4. Benjamin Franklin. 1706-1790. American Scientist, Publisher, Diplomat.
5. Luke 23: 34.
6. John Bankston. 2003. *Henry Ford and the Assembly Line.*
7. "The Rise and Fall of the Spartans." The History Channel.
8. Government Printing Office. 1973. *Committee on Veterans' Affairs. U.S. Senate, Medal of Honor Recipients: 1863-1973.* Washington, D.C.
9. John 3: 16.

Chapter 16

1. University of Dayton. 2003. *Student Handbook.*
2. *Brothers and Sisters to Us,* 1979.
3. *Character Counts! The Josephson Institute of Ethics.* March 2004.
4. Roy B. Basler (Ed.). August 1, 1858. *The Collected Works of Abraham Lincoln,* Volume II.
5. David Halbertstam. April 18, 2004. "Shall We Overcome?" *Parade.*
6. John Wooden, 1997. *Wooden: A Lifetime of Reflections On and Off the Court.*
7. John Wooden. 2003. *They Call Me Coach.*

Chapter 17

1. Michael Reagan. 1998. *The Common Sense of an Uncommon Man: The Wit, Wisdom, and Eternal Optimism of Ronald Reagan.*
2. Ibid.
3. Ibid.
4. Matthew 5: 6.
5. "Peace for Our Time," speech by Neville Chamberlain, September 30, 1938, 10 Downing Street after his arrival home from the infamous Munich Conference of 1938.
6. Michael Les Benedict. 1999. *The Impeachment and Trial of Andrew Johnson.*
7. Loren Eiseley. 1979. *The Star Throwers.*

Name Index

Acton, Lord 121
Abdul-Jabbar, Kareem 211
Andreotta, Glenn 62
Antoinette, Marie 119
Arafat, Yasser 44
Augustine, Norm 105
Ayers, Steve 30
Bankston, John 240
Bannister, Roger 85
Barrie, James 161
Beethoven 196
Benedict, Michael 240
Bennett, William 236
bin Laden, Osama 44
Bonds, Barry 92
Boomer, Walter 100–01
Boyer, Charles 59
Bryant, James 22–23
Buckley, Reid 236
Burgess, Lee 170
Burke, Arleigh 14–15
Burns, Ken 236
Burlingame, Charles "Chic" 45–47
Bush, George W. 43, 232
Cabana, Robert 24, 38–39
Caesar, Augustus 181
Caesar, Julius 71
Calvert, James 235
Capone, Al 36–7
Carter, Jimmy 148–49
Carter, Rosalyn 149

Chamberlain, Joshua L. 32–34, 39
Chamberlain, Neville 223
Chopin 196
Churchill, Winston 128
Colburn, Lawrence 62
Comen, Ben 133–34
Condon, John 12-13
Covey, Stephen 67, 98
Cox, Archibald 62, 108
Culbertson, Frank 46–48
Custer, George Armstrong 101
Darwin, Charles 109
de Tocqueville, Alexis 145
Decatur, Stephen 53
Dickens, Charles 220
DiMaggio, Joe 92
Dmetruk, Steve 171
Donne, John 190, 195
Edison, Thomas 161
Eisenhower, Dwight "Ike" 98
Eiseley, Loren 225
Enright, Joe 39
Evers, Medgar 208
Fisher, Molly 92–93
Filton, Robert 236
Ford, Henry 84, 195
Fox, George 144
Frankl, Viktor 97, 99–100, 107, 149–51
Franklin, Ben 131, 190
Frye, Scott 49
Gandhi, Mahatma 156, 159–60, 212, 218
Gavin, Jim 174–75
Gonzales, James 103–104
Goode, Alexander 144
Greenstreet, Lionel 179
Gretzky, Wayne 92

Harper, Greg 171
Hale, Nathan 43
Hay, Willard "Dub" 21
Hearn, Chester 237
Hecomovich, Michael 10, 22
Helmsley, Leona 120
Henderson, Joe 172–74
Herbert, George 227
Holtz, Lou 188
Horry, Robert 86
Howe, Dave 206
Howe, Gordy 92
Hurley, Frank 178
Iacocca, Lee 129, 188
Jackman, Michele 91
Jackson, Phil 117
James, Michael 171
Jenkins, Don 220
Jervis, Lord Admiral John 25
Jesus 68, 119, 132, 142, 181–83, 189, 191
Johnson, Andrew 225
Jones, John Paul 29
Jordan, Michael 208
Kant, Immanuel 204
Keating, Timothy 48–50
Kehoe, Michael 11–12
Keller, Helen 160
Kennedy, John F. 141,144–45, 225
King, Martin Luther 25, 108, 127, 135, 208, 218
Koskimaki, George 238
Kouzes, James 235
Kremian, F. Terry 143
Krulak, Charles 176–77
Lawrence, William 20
Leahy, Frank 212
Lee, Robert E. 33, 73, 106, 159, 166, 196–97, 218

Leonidas, King 165, 197
Lewis, C.S. 31
Liehard, John 109–10
Lincoln, Abraham 25, 68, 134, 156, 166, 191, 196, 208, 216
Lombardi, Vince 118-19
Long, Luz 146
Manchester, William 239
Mantle, Mickey 92, 187–88, 199
Maury, Matthew 109
Mays, Willie 92
McCandless, Dean 174–75
McCloy, John 164
Meredith, James 108
Metzger, James 9, 13–14, 22, 49-50
Miller, Dennis 156
Montor, Karl 235
Moses 190
Mozart 196
Nelson, Dan 58
Nelson, Lord 72, 197
Nichols, Bruce 23
Nixon, Richard 62, 108, 120
Nouwen, Henry 102
Novak, William 236
O'Brien, Tom 59
O'Hare, Butch 34–36, 39
O'Hare, Eddie 36–38, 39
Owens, Jesse 146–47
Parker, Chuck 133
Parks, Rosa 108, 208, 226
Patton, George S. 29, 31
Perkins, Dennis 239
Perot, H. Ross 20
Pershing, John 122
Poling, Clark 144
Posner, Barry 235

Powell, Colin 51, 171, 209
Poyer, Dave 195
Presley, Elvis 206
Ptak, Alan 104–05
Puller, Chesty 166
Reagan, Michael 240
Reagan, Ronald 171, 217
Reilly, Rick 238
Rice, Condoleeza 209
Richardson, Elliot 62, 108
Rickey, Branch 107
Robinson, Jackie 107
Rockne, Knute 212
Roosevelt, Theodore 32
Roosevelt, Franklin D. 43
Rose, Pete 25
Rowe, Curtis 211
Ruckelshaus, William 108
Ruggero, Ed 239
Ruth, Babe 88
Sampras, Pete 87
Sattler, John 49–50
Scott, Sir Walter 19
Shackleton, Ernest 177–80
Shakespeare, William 19, 115
Singer, Marcus 203
Smith, Captain 73
Stagg, Alonzo 210–11, 213
Staubach, Roger 157
Stewart, James 86
Stockdale, James 171
Stuart, Jeb 73
Teresa, Mother 147–48, 156, 212, 218
Thatcher, Margaret 196
Thomas, Cal 15–16
Thompson, Hugh 62

Thompson, John 239
Tilden, Samuel 164
Truman, Harry 107–08
Twain, Mark 71
Tzu, Lao 167
Wallace, William 166
Walton, Bill 118, 211
Washington, George 145, 226
Washington, John 144
Weaver, Christopher 48
Webb, James 235
Weinberger, David 113
Welch, Jack 171
Winfrey, Oprah 209
Wilson, Frank 236
Winter, John 102
Wooden, John 89, 118, 158, 210–12
Wooden, Joshua 210
Woods, Tiger 92
Xerxes, King 165–66

BOOKS FROM ACADEMY LEADERSHIP PUBLISHING

The Leader's Compass: Set Your Course for Leadership Success
(2003, ISBN: 0-9727323-0-6, $14.95) by Ed Ruggero and
Dennis F. Haley

*The Corporate Compass: Providing Focus and Alignment to Stay
the Course*
(2005, ISBN: 0-9727323-3-0, $17.95) by Ed Ruggero and
Dennis F. Haley

Inspiring Leadership: Character and Ethics Matter
(2005, ISBN: 0-9727323-2-2, $24.95) by R. Stewart Fisher and
Perry J. Martini

Academy Leadership books are available at special quantity discounts to use as premiums and sales promotions, or for use in corporate training programs. For more information, please call Academy Leadership at 866-783-0630, visit www.academyleadership.com, or write to: 10120 Valley Forge Circle, King of Prussia, PA 19406 USA.